THE ALHAMBRA

The hill which serves as its pedestal ending at the east with the Cerro del Sol (Hill of the Sun), Between the Alhambra and the Silla del Moro (Moor's Seat) and the Generalife, is the valley called «Aikaibia», now known as the Slope of the Death or of the Rey chico (Little King).

On the north side of this triangle is the river Darro, the western end finishing at the Alcazaba and the south with «Handaq as Sabika» (the Moat of Melted Silver), whence we find the present central entrance through the forest and the Hill of Mauror with the Vermillion Towers.

The hill where the Alhambra stands, it's top more than seven hundred meters above the sea level, is an eroded formation of the Sierra Nevada mountains, formed of detritus shist and quartz. Although more recent than some of the formations which forms it, even if not proper rock, has by various crystalizations gained the required resistance and stability. If to this stability one adds richness in ferrous materials in the soil, (reason for the red colour), one can understad why the hill has served as a firm, solid pedestal for the castle of the Alhambra for so many centuries.

Shaped like a boat, it's prow formed by the Alcazaba pointing towards the city, with a lenghtof over seven hundred meters from the Alcazaba to the tower of the Cabo de la Carrera and a beam of more than two hundred meters at its widest, giving an area of some thirteen hectares and having a perimeter of over two kilometers of walls and some thirty towers, some of them only ruins.

The very recent publication of the book "Foco de antigua luz sobre la Alhambra" by the eternally young and always surprising Emilio García Gómez, using a text of ibn Aljatib discovered in Rabat, ('Rooting through my saddlebags to entertain myself in my exile'), had caused all existing theories, solid or excentric about the Alhambra, to be shaken as if by an earthquake until the collapse in a thousand pieces, and those held to be 'profound studies of the Alhambra' by they the Sacred Cows of Arabism or Islamic Archaology, or simple studies of Arabic Art which have arisen in past centuries, all are undone by the evidence of a contemprary of Yusef I or his son Muhammed V, the great builders of the Alhambra.

Firstly with the new, unitary view of the monument we have to trow out, at last, all the funtional divisions of Mexuar, Serrallo, Harem, amongst which the Italian word "Serraglio (from the Turkish, via the Persian, meaning "harem" too) is seen as a separate dependency of the private dwelling of the king.

Another point to remember, and often forgotten, is what the Alhambra represents as architecture: this has always been undervalued. We all become tourist when faced with the monument. In the "Manifiesto de la Alhambra" prepared by a group of Spanish architects in 1953, it says «'The Alhambra has never been looked at from the architect's point of view: strangely, even architects who faced with the Escorial sharpen their professional eye, when they arrive at the Alhambra, slacken their perspicacity and become mere curious tourist: even to the extend of excusing their complacency by recourse to their emotions: Yes, I like this, but not as architecture'», (page 11).

Later on pages 13 and 14 of the same text they add: «'The relationship between this XIVth century and the most progressive modern architecture is, in some points, astonishing: the human scale is seen in both, the use of organic asymetry in the composition of levels, the way garden and landscape are related to the building form, the strict economic use of materials, without frills, and in many other ways too numerous to mention'».

Thus, the Alhambra, despite its great age, is in concept and construction an architectural complex of great modernity. To quote a modern architect of recognized prestige, the Swiss architect Le Corbusier found in the monument his definition of modern architecture: «'the intelligent interplay of volumes correctly and magnificently united under the light»' an idea established in his "Cité Moderne" (1922). In his buildings he attemps to bring garden and landscape into interiors, and he always uses the human scale as his module.

In the Alhambra, the harmony of asymmetry, the contrast of light and shace, light reducing mass, the focus in the buildings of sky, water and landscape, the most and lintel structure, «'the agile use of nature in the planing of buildings»' are some of the architectural solutions which add to the modernity.

Prieto Moreno, to whom these last words between inverted commas belong, and who was for many years the Architected Conserver of the Alhambra, says in continuation «'the Alhambra combines in its buildings many architectural concepts which are still valid today, and, of course, they are considered masterpieces»'. Another achievement in construction is the way that perpendicular axis of the courts is mantained, given the irregularity of the site and the different ages of building. This gives the impression of a regular and harmonic whole.

Francisco Pí y Margall assures us, the Alhambra «'grew century by century, and every day increased in splendour»'. In effect, the Alhambra was not planned from the beginning as a union of various constructions, rather it grew from the citadel which existed at the end of the IXth century. This sufficed, (in 1238), as the residence of Muhammad ben Yusef ben Nasr, lord of Arjona. When the kingdom of Granada began to grow in importance, that citadel was insufficient for a real king: starting with the old castle Nasr and mosques, schools, etc. until it became a palatial city capable of housing an increasing and aristocratic population.

There was at the end of the reign of Muhammad ben Nasr —who helped Fernando III in the conquest of Seville in 1248—, a period of peace based on a truce with the Castillians. At the same time diplomatic and administrative needs increased in a kingdom which covered territory from Gibraltar to the frontier with Murcia, joined to the sea by a coastal line from ancient Calpe to the river Almanzora, and including the provinces of Granada, Almería and Málaga, with parts of Jaén, Córdoba, Seville and Cádiz, a long frontier marked by a number of towns still called "de la Frontera".

A century later during the reigns of the great builders Yusuf I and his son Muhammad V —especially at the end of the later reign— the Alhambra, seen from the Albayzín, was a white castle on a plinth of vegetation reaching down to the river Darro. This forest that served as a zoological garden where the animals ran free, was viewed from the innumerable windows of the palace. From the farms and country houses of the Vega (plane) then a forest of fruit groves which concealed a population almost equal to that of the city (according to Andrea Navaggiero), the Alhambra stood out white and brilliant in the setting sun, like a flash of golden light on the terraced gardens of the Generalife and Cerro del Sol and at its far background Ŷabal Šulayr al-Talŷ (the Mountain of the Sun and Snow, Sierra Nevada) framed by the blu sky.

But, if the Alhambra was white, why was it called "La Roja", (the Red)? We venture a personal hypothesis, that the name «Hamra» (The red) was given as an analogy of the family name of the founder of the dynasty, «al Ahmar», tha is

"The Red", and this name became a common-place in the XIVth century.

The white rendering can clearly be seen on those walls and towers which have not suffered major restoration: these conserve areas, large or small, of the original finish. Finally we draw attention to the use of the name Moslem instead of Arab when speaking of the ancient inhabitants of the «Madina al-Hamra'». Arab implies to a certain extent a nationality, and the creators of this Medieval Wonder were Spanish, grand children and great grand children of Spaniards, who spoke Arabic and practiced Islam; the product of a happy fusion of races who were the founders of a culture which has no equal.

To present this book to the reader we recall the words of F. Villaespesa, from Almería, dedicated to the Alhambra, and may be seen on a plaque near the Puerta de las Granadas:

«'Thought not even a shadow of the walls remain, the memory of the place is eternal, a unique refuge for dreams and artistry.

Then the last nightingale, which breaths upon the Earth will comme to build his nest and sing his songs, like a last farewell, amongst the glorious ruins of the Alhambra».

THE GATE OF JUSTICE

oday this is almost the only entrance to the walled enclosure of the *Madina Al-Hamra* (The City of the Alhambra). It is a square shaped tower joined on one side to the wall which enclosed the aristocratic city known today as the Alhambra, and it is without any doubt, the most important doorway to the monument.

A spandrel of white marble decorated with plaques and strapwork painted green sits above the segmented lintel over the inner arch, where one can see a symbolic key —of which more later—, and below a copy of a gothic Virgin Mary, one can see in a beautiful inscribed panel of arabesque characters: "This Gate called bab al-sari'a was ordered put up, may God make the justice of islam prosper and be a sign of His glory for a long time, by the Emir of the Moslems, the warrior Sultan and Just, Abu-l-Hayyay-Yusuf [...]". This work was completed in the month of the Glorious Nativity of the year 749". That is june 1348, the same year that Giovanni Bocaccio wrote his "Decameron" while isolated in a country villa to escape the terrible "Black Death" which sweapt Europe and which shortly, like an apocaliptic blow, would reach our peninsula as the "The Great Slaughter" causing massive loss of life in Andalucía, with particular virulence the city of Almería where, in seven months two thirds of the population were wipped out.

The name Gate of Justice could be supported by the part of the inscription which says "May God make the justice of Islam prosper within her"*.

As to the name 'Gate of the Esplanade', this refers to the existence of an esplanade prior to the building of the roads to the Generalife and the forest.

The open hand incised on the key-stone of this first arch has given rise to many theories as to its significance. At first, and from long ago, the open hand with the palm forward was a sign of peace: it is the natural posture at the approach of an enraged rival. But, in this case, it seems the significance is in the five fingers, what the Muslims call *al-Hamza* (the five), that is the five fundamental precepts of Islam: believe in one God, prayer, alms giving, fasting and the pilgrimage to Mecca.

Some see in this hand, and in relation with the key on the second arch, a talismanic significance. There abound in the kingdom of Granada great number of these symbols, specially the key symbol, on both pottery and buildings.

At the level of the roof terrace there are two gargoyles, that in time of war could support a gallery or barbican and in this way covered any blind angles around the tower.

Behind this outer arch, which due to its massive size never had doors, is a separation or defensive well —typical of the innovative nazarite military architecture—, in which for hurling down boiling oil or melted lead from above.

This second arch, made of marble, as is the whole archway, probably was polychromed in the Hispano-Musulman period. It is decorated with a shell above the key-stone, and other two at the same height at the edge of the spandrels. The arch is decorated with vaussoir, alternately raised, rest on columns with cubic capitals and koranic inscriptions. At the center of the arch, on the key-stone, one sees a key with tassels. This has given rise, like the hand itself, to numerous theories; Hurtado de Mendoza, according Gallego y Burín, opined that this was the emblem of the kings of Granada. One can, of course, see this key and tassel over the nearby "Wine Gate" and over the entrance to the Generalife from the lower gardens. it seems that the "Gate of Seven Floors" —demolished—, had the same motif. Basilio Pavón has collected evidence of other keys on the entrance of *mudejar* palaces in Tordesillas, which Further up is an inscription giving the date of construction, and over this a nich where a copy of a gothic Virgin is displayed. The Catholic Monarchs, whose emblems are on the plinth, ordered the original made in 1501 by Ruperto Aleman.

The nich refered to above is carved out of a panel of exquisite mosaic of rombuses, in white and blue, of similar manufactured to those on the outer arch of the tower.

Beyond this doorway is a horse-shoe arch of dressed stone on half columns, carved into the frame, with cubic capitals. Between the two arches are hung the iron clad gates, which retain their original lock and bolts. We enter under these arches into the access corridor of four right-angle turns in the *Almohade* style, covered by squinched vaults. These are much in keeping with the military character of the entrance, each turn becoming a point of defence.

On the left-hand wall of the corridor one can see three recesses with benches for the guards, a military detail repeated in the other entrances to the Alhambra. Above them, at different hwight on the wall, there are racks for some hundred lances of various lenghts. To judge by the lenght of one of them, they are from the late XVth Century or early XVI^{th14}.

On the wall opposite the exit, in one of the niches used as a bench for the guards in olden times, in 1588 the residents of the Alhambra set up an altar for the veterans of the garrison. This altar, with a canvas of the Virgin Mary and Child by Diego de Navas, is seldom mentioned in books on the Alhambra for it is generally closed and because its poor quality.

However, the cisterns were built in 1494, the plaque must

4

have been set up some years later and have been nearer to the cisterns mentioned. Very curious is the confusion as to the name of the Moorish monarch reigning at the time of the surrender, more so given the proximity to the event.

We finally emerge through the rear archway, discovered by Rafael Contreras in 1588.

The outer face of this arch still preserves in its spandrels remains of mosaic, similar to those on the inner arch with the nich of the Virgin. They rest on a two centred arch of typical Hispano-Musulman style, and are decorated with a blind tracery of much restored bricks. The infilling of the romboids is different to that of the outer gate.

To the north side of the gate is an inner moat, which extended all round the walls of the Alhambra at times covered, others open, but always deep enough to allow cavalry patrols.

The opposite wall, with one's back to the gate, has a rampart which runs from the top of the tower. This wall which seems to have collapsed in the early XVIth. Century was rebuilt with grave stones; possibly from the nearby cemetry of Maqabir al-Assal - at the foot of the modern Barranco del Abogado, above the Campo del Príncipe. or, perhaps, from the Yabbanat Bab-al Fajjarin (Potters Gate Cemetry) which according to Ibn Aljatib *'was placed mext to the gobernor's residence'*, that is the royal cemetry of al-Fajjarin to the south of the Alhambra above the Jewish quarter of Mauror near Torres Bermejas. These stones are poor stuff, rough hewn with inscriptions of cufic characters of the edges. Their poverty contrast with the marbel burial stones of the royal family, conserved in the Museo Hispano-Musulmán. Found in the Royal Rawda (cemetry), inside the Palace, coloured and guilded, they lead to the belief that the ones in the wall have a more humble origin.

LA ALCAZABA
(The citadel)

The similarity between the Alcazaba of the Alhambra and the Alcazar of Segovia —two military spurs cutting into the city— does not seem to be merely fortuitous rather it is the adaptation of military buildings to the characteristics of the site.

The rivers Genil an Darro —the first rather more to the south— perform with respect to the Alcazaba and City of the Alhambra the same function that the Eresma and the Clamores rivers do respect to the Alcazar and City of Segovia. Both fortresses rise on a promontory some eighty meters above the plane and both face west.

The Alcazaba injustly forgotten by those who wrote about Granada after the conquest, blinded by the Alcazares of the Nazarite, is the embryo from which the aristocratic city — later called *Madina al-Hamrá*— is born.

During the civil wars of the IXth century and the battles against invading Almoravides and Almohades it was known under different names until after the XIIIth century the name *Qa'lat al Hamra'* (Red Castle) became commonplace as the same it carries to this day.

From the top of the *Torre de la Vela* (Watching Tower) one can clearly see two enclosures, one within the other. The smaller inner one is probably of Roman origin, as can be deduced from the foundations visible in the lower part of the walls, and *Califal* as it was rebuilt in 889 by the *qaysi* Sawwar ben Handum during the defense of this fortress against the Mozárabes and the Muladíes of Umar ben Hafsum.

Even after the arrival in Granada of Muhammad ben Nasr Al-Ahmar in 1238, the Alcazaba was for many years an isolated castle separated from the are to the east, where the royal palaces were later to be built, by a profound ditch. In the time of Yusuf I a curtain of walls and towers was rised over this, the remains of which can still be seen in the *Plaza de los Aljibes* (Water cisterns Court); one of these towers was used as a filter for the cisterns which the Conde de Tendilla ordered to bouilt in 1494 thus filling in the ditch.

King Yusuf I was also responsible for the joining of the royal palaces to the Alcazaba with a wall and inner passage, to which one ascended by a stair which still exists in the *Tower of Tahona* —rediscovered in 1955 beneath the *Cubo de la Alhambra,* —that is a renaissance construction, pot bellied and with no projection in order to reduce the effects of artillery fire, a weapon which was beginning to be useful at that time.

It would seen that Muhammad ben Nasr al-Ahmar was the builder of the Torre de la Vela at the western end. It has a height ot twently seven meters and a side of sixteen motors. Its four stories have been much altered to adapt them as living space, above all in the lower floor, thus the appearance of the interior is changed and the stairs have been moved. The tower has also lost some of its original height when the battlements were removed, generally due to the desasters it suffered since the XVIth century: first an earthquake (1522), them the explosion of the power factory in the Darro Valley (1590) —which left it in a sorry state—, and finally because a thunderbolt in 1882 which destroyed the belfry in its original position, the nort corner of the tower.

The bell which was recast in 1773, replacing the original one, has the function of controlling the watering of the Vega. On more tragic occasions it call the city to the alert, as wen the Alhambra caught fire in 1890.

From the excellent viewpoint of the tower platform one ca see to the north the ancient district of the Albaicin, and to the east the gipsy quarter of the Sacromonte awaiting a promised restoration these last twenty years. Above this is the *Hermitage of St. Michael 'a domesticated Archangel in the twelve o'clock position'* which stands in the old walls of the city of Granada that "pour" into the valley, bearing the scars of centuries. The murmur of the Albaicín can be heard across the brutal roar of the traffic. In the spring time the Albaicin is enveloped by the perfume of flowers which when one is far from the city, still pervades in the memory. All this is divided from the Alhambra by the Valley of the Darro, which extends to the right into the incredible *Valparaíso* (Paradise Valley) which has the perfume of fresh strawberries and the freshness of clean spring water. This is the Granada that Gautier described as *'a celestial Jerusalem'* and what Al-Saqundi, from Cordoba, described as *'a pasture for the eyes and an elevation for the soul'*.

To the west spreads the modern city. To the south is the *Hill of Mauror* with the *Vermillion Towers,* a most ancient structure which protected the military camp ther ant the dungeons for the prisioners. To the left of this is the *Carmen de Rodríguez Acosta,* modern, white and cold. More to the left is the architectural cocktail of the Alhambra Palace Hotel and in the far distance, where the earth meets the sky, is the *Suspiro del Moro* (The Sigh of the Moor) and the last hillocks of the Sierra Nevada, its highest point to the south is covered of snow for most of the year; the iron coloured foothills are peppered with romanticalley named villages. Near, to the east side, stands the stony imperial architecture of Charles V and in the distance, at the foot of the *Cerro del Sol* (Hill of the Sun), stands the *Generalife,* the "garden without equal". There cipresses, like earthés fingers, thrust skywards beggins for peace and silence for this landscape.

If one looks downwards, on the western side, one spies a military structure shaped like a Phrygian cap, its point turned towards the river Darro: this is the *Baluarte* (The Bulwark), a XVth century work made as a gun platform facing the city and is the real "prow" of the Alcalzaba. The city of the Alhambra seems to have feared the population of Granada more than some outside foe. This is the reason that, finding the citadel of the Albaicin encompassed by the surrounding suburbs and cutting of any escape to the countryside, the kings removed themselves to the Red Hill. This though it required major repair and construction, offered ample means of escape to the outside if flight became necessary, other than at the western end: the Alhambra was entirely outside the enclosure of Granada.

On the south side, starting from the bulwark, runs the *Camino Militar* (Soldiers Way) which crosses the *Bab Handac* (The Ravine Gate) which was demolished in 1526 to build the *Puerta de las Granadas* (Pomegranates Gate). In the same period the Cuesta de Gomérez was opened upt in order to give direct access from Plaza Nueva to the central road of what is now the forest of the Alhambra. This Camino Militar joined with Torres Bermejas and the encampments located beside this castle, allowing the main garrison in the Alcazaba to be reinforced from there. The wall continued down to Granada enclosing her within a spacious bailey defended by a number of castles and forts.

Before the building of the Puerta de las Granadas the entry to the Alhambra began in the *Plaza de Cuchilleros* (Cutlers Square); zig-zagging through the districts of *La Churra* and Almanzora, one entered the fortifyed gate Bab Handac, and along the edge of the ravine of As-Sabika arrived at the *Gate of Justice.* Until the building of The Bulwark this urban way could doorway. Filled and uncovered again in 1857, this doorway can be seen near the south foot of the Torre de la Vela.

The Puerta de las Armas (Gate of Arms) which is the true main gateway to the Alcazaba, was equipped with a portcullis its raising and lowering controlled from the floor immediately above the entrance. One reached there along the walled road of the Alcazaba: this tower is attached to the bailey of the Alcazaba and next to the Vela. The entrance to the Torre de la Armas is a wide passage which turns sharp right to meet a large space —certainly the guardsé room— where the way opens in two directions: one to the left leading to the royal palace and the other to the right which give entry to the Alcazaba. The visitor to the royal residences —whether on horse back or on foot— was required to go some ninety meters with his right side exposed to the crossbowmen on the inner wall —the shield was born on the left side—. Passing first a gate, since demolished, one came to the next point of control at the *Torre de la Tahona* and then to a market or *zoco* (its remains can still be seen) which was held by tradition in the entrance of all fortified cities.

At the end of a pebble paved slope our visitor arrived in the *Plaza de las Armas.* Before his gaze was now a central street with a bath house for the soldiers to his left. On both sides were houses for the officers of the garrison, armorers, blacksmiths, etc. the foundations of which are still to be seen. There are also water cisterns, ovens and dungeon.

This Plaza de las Armas is enclosed by the following towers, starting from the Torre de la Vela: Torre and Puerta de las Armas, *Alquiza, El Criado del Dr. Ortiz* (The servant of Dr. Ortiz), and in the north west corner, la *Torre del Homenaje* (The Donjon), similar in height to the Torre de la Vela an irregular in plan (12.12 × 10.45 mts.). Its five floors, including the cellars, served first as the residence for the wardens and then as a prison for Algerian pirates and francophiles.

According to Don Luis Seco de Lucena the Torre del Homenaje is one of the oldest in the Alcazaba, dating from the period of the Caliphate. An archaeological study of the materials of which it is constructed compared with those at its base, leads one to think that perhaps Al-Ahmar ordered it to be rebuilt on the ruins of a tower dating from the nineth century.

After the Torre del Homenaje comes the *Torre Quebrada* (Cracked Tower) so called because of the long crack to be seen frm the Plaza de los Aljibes, looking like a wound from head to toe. It is solid to the top of the wall, having two floors above this level. Next comes the *Torre del Adarguero* (Leather-shield Maker) of which only the shell remains. To the right of the Torre del Adarguero is the former entrance to the Alcazaba which leads directly to the *Jardín del Adarve.* This garden is the old moat which divided the inner and outher baileys and was filled in with rubble and earth in the early XVIIth century by the Marqués de Mondéjar, to make the garden. The original moat depth can be imagined by observing the height of the cipresses planted at the foot of the outer wall.

On the inner wall there were two smal towers, of which only the *Torre de la Sultana* remains. Through this garden going west, one reaches the *Torre de la Polvora* (Gunpowder Tower) which marks the start of the above mentioned Camino Militar to Torres Bermejas. From here, through another small tower, one enters the Torre de la Vela by a modern entrance at the level of the second floor.

From either the Adarve gardens or from the Torre de la Pólvora the view is so espectacular that any description can only diminish it.

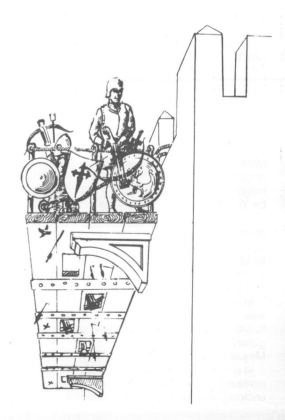

THE OLD ROYAL PALACE

THE HALL OR ROOM OF THE MEXUAR

This is without doubt the part of the palace which has suffered most from conversions, almost always at the instigation of the Christian Governors in the service of their King, adapting it to new uses and functions, drastically altering the original appearance.

These changes have meant the complete destruction of old structures, making it difficult to identify the original entrances to this part of the palace, where it seems the council met to decide important judicial matters.

Those approaching from Granada, once they passed the filter of the Alcazaba and the control of the Tahona Tower, found themselves in a town square, or Zoco, a typical feature of town entrances —and the Alhambra was a town. They then passed into a higher courtyard defended, on the left, by a tower called the Tower of Mohamed (also known as Hontiveros or of the Chickens), where they found, in front and to the left, the Alminar of a small mosque. In front of our supposed visitor a flight of steep steps breaks the pace of his walk, because of the difficulty in climbing them. Finally he reached the Court of Machuca.

This court is so called because of the Machuca Tower on the side facing the River Darro, where the architect of the Palace of Charles V., and his son Luis (also an Architect) lived. On the opposite side was a twin of this gallery but only some ruins on the floor remain. Its original form is recalled by some cypress arches.

The entrance to the buildings was very similar to the present one. A flight of ruined stairs at the end of the cypress gallery seems to confirm this. In the small upper court we find the entrance to the Hall of the Mexuar.

This doorway, with its fine carved surrounds was, according to Seco de Lucena, brought from some other location.

This room, commonly called the MEXUAR is probably the oldest part of the royal apartments to survive, even if it was much altered in the time of Yusuf I and his son Mohamed V. In a freeze of a what was a roof light at the centre of the room, one can read *"Glory to our lord Abu-l-Walid Ismail"*. This and its similarities to the Generalife, built and decorated by this King, lead to the belief that it was built in the early XIVth century.

Inside on the left side of the south wall one can see some archaeological "cuts" which reveal a dado over one and a half meters from the floor. This belongs to an earlier construction, and is also similar to the painted dados of the Generalife. This earlier palace was probably abandoned by Ismail's descendants because of the problem of raising water to that height. The new building was constructed at the present level by Yusuf or his son.

In plan there is a notable disproportion between the areas divided by the central columned area, the northern end, between the columns and the entrance being much the larger. In Machuca's plan, in the place now occupied by the columns of a gallery, we see a wall which enclosed the room in a square of two equal halves.

In this room a chapel was installed. Designed in 1537, it was not completed until the XVIIth century. As the room was found to be too small the end was demolished and a choir gallery built with access stairs up the wall of the court of the Mexuar, in the space gained with the pick.

In a recent excavation a small court with clay paviours was revealed under the choir gallery, proving that the room was enclosed at this side. However it still remains to be proved if there was another little door at the east end of the demolished wall which communicated with the small courtyard as shown on the drawing.

One reached this court through a door from the court of Machuca, probably where the window in the northwest corner is. In this way the Mexuar was isolated from those whose business in the palace was not related to it, direct access being through the door in the south wall.

From the small court and via a narrow doorway of moulded plaster on the east side one passes to a gallery leading to the adjacent Golden Room, (this door has lost some of its height because the floor has been raised to that of the rest of the room).

The four columns at the centre of the room indicate the location of a roof lantern, similar in design to that of the rest room of the baths in the Palace of Comares. It would have had clerestory lights on all four sides, filtering the daylight through coloured glass. Below this, in the square formed by the four columns, the Council met to decide important judicial matters.

Luis del Marmol who, at the start of the XVIIth century must have had more recent information about the palaces, stated that it was in this room *"where the King called his council"* and in the doorway there was a tile which said *"Enter and fear not to ask for justice, for you will find it"*.

When the warden's residence (now the Hispano-Musulman Museum) was built above, the lantern was destroyed. The square space which remained, enclosed by the four columns, was covered with a radial wooden ceiling. The west wall was thickened to take the extra weight, and the large, iron grilled windows which now light the room were opened in it. It is impossible to know what the outside of this wall looked like.

When the chapel was built the door was blocked up and a marble altar set up in its place between the tiled pillars of Hercules with the motto "non plus ultra" (not far beyond).

As we have said the room was extended to include the small court. In the dividing line a choir Gallery was built, supported by a decorated beam resting on Arabic columns, with their bases sunk in the floor. To this was added a wooden railing and two more columns of the same style which reached the ceiling. The Moorish Oratory behind was used as a sacristy, a door being opened into the adjacent court of The Mexuar, in the north wall of what was the small court.

Despite all these viscisitudes the upper part of the walls of the hall conserve the original colour and gilding of the plaster decoration, and some of the wooden ceilings are original, recognisable by their polychroming and darker colour. The whole room, including the part added on, has a dado of XVIth century Moorish tiles, in the central stars of which we can see alternately the emblems of the Nasar dynasty, Cardinal Mendoza, the Austrian Two-Headed Eagle, and the columns of Hercules from the imperial crest.

Above this work in ceramics (which lacks the brightness of the work it imitates), the length and breadth of the room we can read the litanies *"The power of God"*, *"The glory of God"*, and *"The kingdom of God"*.

Of the ceramic columns at the sides of the altar, the one covering the doorway was removed to the east wall, together with the basin for holy water. A plaster imperial crown can still be seen over the doorway, but the other one remains as it was on top of the column.

THE ORATORY OF THE MEXUAR

As we have seen this is to be found at the end of the hall of the Mexuar, facing the Albaicin. It was one of the parts of the Alhambra which suffered most damage from the explosion of 1590, so much so that it had to be completely rebuilt at the time, this work being completed in 1917.

On any plan of the Alhambra one can see that the Oratory does not follow the line of the walls. On the contrary, from the end of the gallery of the tower of Machuca (the original entrance) it angles sharply to the south east, seeking orientation towards Mecca for the Mihrab.

In the north wall are four windows, of which three are aljimeces, with delicate marble columns and alabaster capitals. Below the windows, level with the floor of the Mihrab is a narrow bench which replaced the original floor when this was lowered to bring it in line with that of the under choir or to make the window tops coincide with the height of a standing Christian.

Nowadays the oratory is no more than a marvellous place from which to view the Albaycin. The unreliability of the restoration which it has suffered leads it to be ignored, except for some inscriptions around the Mihrab, referring to Muhammad V, and one that says, *"Be not neglectful, come ye to pray"*, which given their content could be copied from the originals.

THE COURT OF THE MEXUAR

This is a small court which, for no apparent reason, was called "The Court of The Mosque", in days gone by. On the north side is the *Cuarto Dorado* and opposite the impressive front which has been held until now to be the entrance to the Palace of Comares.

One has only to see the many engravings of this court made in the last century, to lose any reticence about the work of the restorer. In this case the restorations are numerous and well executed.

Fortunately all these "pastiches" were removed, during the successive works of restoration started in the time of the Contreras family. The last to go was the heavy, white painted arch, demolished in "The Year of Intelligent Restorations of 1965".

The court centres on a fluted, white marble fountain. This is a replica placed there in 1943 to fill the hole left by the removal in 1626 of the original one used as part of the Christian fountain in the Court of Lindaraja.

The demolition of the Morisco arch and the removal of the projecting floor which it supported has restored the former attractiveness of the Cuarto Dorado gallery. This gallery is composed of three well proportioned arches which rest on white marble capitals, possibly Almohade in origin. These in turn rest on slender white marble columns. The capitals are a stylised version, inspired by the zoomorphic capitals of Persepolis.

The *Cuarto Dorado* (Golden Room) beyond the gallery opens onto the woods through a Gothic window, divided by a mullion on whose head are the emblems of the Reyes Catolicos (Catholic Monarchs). The restoration dates from their reign and the original ceiling was preserved but redecorated with Gothic motifs. The ceiling rests on a frieze containing the emblems and motto of the royal couple. On the ceiling, restored in 1965, is a wealth of gilding, fully justifying the ancient name of this room.

On the eastern wall of the court is a tunnel which leads to the Baths of the Palace of Comares it has rooms on boths sides, once used as quarters for the guards and now used to store the results of the excavations being carried out in the Alhambra.

THE FAÇADE OF THE PALACE OF COMARES

To many authors this façade, on the south wall of the court,

Deduces the "existence of some architectural or decorative element in the court, to give the correct orientation". It is clear that this façade, intended as the entrance to the Palace of Comares, is far too monumental for this small dark courtyard.

A study of the manuscript by Ibn Aljatib, discovered in Rabat has lead don Emilio García Gómez to surmise that this façade, together with its doors, was originally sited on the southern side of the Patio de los Arrayanes and that it was the principal entrance to the Palace de Comares, but on the outside. Later, through the records of building works in the Archivo de la Alhambra, he shows that in effect it was moved between 1537 and 1538 to its present location.

However, in Machuca's plan —to which we refer repeatedly in the text— one sees two doors, which confirms Graber's hypothesis on the "existence of some architectural or decorative element to give the correct orientation".

The façade stands on a plinth of three marble steps and the moulded plaster decoration increases in complexity as it rises, perhaps in imitation of the classical orders. It finishes with finely-carved, overhanging eaves, a fine work of carpentry, and rests on a frieze of the same material where decoration is no less perfect thant the eaves or the rafters that supports.

This façade, much restored in the nineteenth century, has dividing strips between the decorative panels. There are an abundance of Magrebies characters surrounding the ajimez windows at the sides and a central window where we see repeated the dynastic motto "Only God is Victor". In the frame around the doors, including the plaster jambs and the panel between the two, one can see various religious themes taken from the Koran written in cufic characters.

Above the lintels of the doors we can see the remains of the original tiling which has been continued in modern stucco down the jambs to the tile dado at the foot of the wall, also restored.

The aesthetic impression of this façade, wherever it was, must have been very moving: polychromed like a Persian carpet, with the mouldings and the eaves gilded, the polished bronze doors also looking like gold.

The right hand door leads to a post-conquest lobby, to some other Christian buildings and finally to the exit from the Arab palace. The left hand door leads to a small room with its ceiling and frieze gilded in the time of the Catholic Monarchs. Here in Gothic characters it erroneously says that Granada was conquered one year before it actually was (in 1492). At the end of its angled corridor we reach the Patio de los Arrayanes.

THE PALACE OF COMARES

THE COURT OF MYRTLES

This complex containing the Hall of Ambassadors or the throne room is the most important of all the buildings in the Alhambra. The austerity of its desing and the balance of its proportions fill the court with a serene majesty, so that one can breathe in the noble grandeur of the kings who built it.

The proportions are just perfect, so much so that when attemps are made to copy them on a smaller scale the effect is paltry, not to say ridiculous.

The Court of Myrtles was the centre of the diplomatic and political activity of the Alhambra, and probably the place of state reception for foreign ambassadors. It would be the place where important visitors would have awaited their turn to be received by the Sultan.

In the recently published book by don Antonio Enrique, "La Alhambra Hermética", the layout of this palace is compared with that of the Temple of Solomon and found to be almost identical. The only differences in the temple built by Hiram Abi are that the entrance was in the position occupied by the Hall of the Ambassadors in the Alhambra, and the *hecat* (or sanctuary) which leads into the *debir* (Holy of Holies) is in the place of the central north window of the Hall of the Ambassadors where the throne was. The columns of *Boaz* and *Jaquin* (Jaquimboaz - may he live forever!) are on the superimposed plans to the left and right of the central north window of the Hall of the Ambassadors.

Our friend and companion Ramón Hernández Macías who died recently had another idea about the palace. He believed that the layout of the palace was like a diagram of the human body. The thinking head was the Hall of the Ambassadors with the brain in the place of the throne. The east and west alcoves, which he pictured occupied by important civil servants or ministers, were the eyes and ears of the brain. The aisles to the left and right of the court which were for the minor officials were the arms that carried out the orders of the brain. The great pool in the middle, a reflection of the infinite sky above and below, was the soul of the diagramatic body.

Until now the whole building has been attributed to Yusuf I. Despite the presence of a eulogy to Muhammad V on the north gallery celebrating his reconquest of Algeciras all the building works belongs to his father's reign. However in Emilio Gómez's study of the afore-mentioned manuscript by Ibn Aljatib it is made clear that the Court of Myrtles belongs to the period of Yusuf I. It was in fact an open esplanade with a central pool. It was left to Muhammad V to enclose this esplanade, converting it into a monumental courtyard and preserving the northern buildings put up by his father, i.e. the gallery and Hall of the Boat (Sala de la Barca), the Tower of Comares with the Hall of the Ambassadors as well as the royal baths below the palace.

Antonio Gallego y Burín is perhaps the only person to have measured the court accurately, piece by piece, and from his precise measurements we have proof of the above assertion. Thus we find that the east and west sides are exactly equal at 36.60 metres, but the north and south sides differ by 0.45 metres being 23.50 metres on the north and 22.95 metres on the south side.

In Antonio Enrique's publication the irregularity of the sides which form a trapezoid is designed "such that the laterals open imperceptibly as one approaches the Throne Room". This gradual unfolding of the Alhambra like a fan opening slowly is something that is repeated time and again and cannot be considered sheer chance.

The medieval visitor who entered from the south, having passed through the main entrance, found before him a huge mirror of water reflecting the white mass of the Tower of Comares and, due to the slope of the white marble floors which permitted the water to reach the bases of the columns on the north side, these appeared to float on the water. All the buildings on this side including the tower became floating palaces. Thus when the rest of Europe was building "castles in Spain, in Granada they built palaces on the water".

The most important function for the pool was that of a mirror, a feature used centuries later (1630-1647) in the well-known Taj Mahal in Agra.

If we suppose that the proponents of the theory about the entrance to The Hall of Comares are correct, the present entrance would have been a secondary entrance from the rooms in the Mexuar, never the solemn entrance to the residence of a king that one would expect.

There are various innovations in the court. The door which now leads to the Court of Lions, for example. Do take a look at the west side of the court opposite the above-mentioned entrance where there are two doors, a wide one and a narrow one, both framed with decorative plaster work. Now look again at the east side of the court where a wide door was put to connect with the Court of Lions in order to break the inexplicable asymmetry with the other side. An entrance was needed here to replace the original one lost when the Palace of Charles V was built.

On many occasions it has been stated that there were no tiled dados along the side walls but that there were some flower beds at ther bases in which jasmin and roses grew. One only has to see the cut-away shape on the lower part of the door surrounds to see that there was a tiled dado at that level. Richard Ford tells us that the daughters of Bucarelli tore down the ceramic tile surrounds that ran the entire length of the court and sold them off. This dado —before it fell victim to the family of that governor of the Alhambra— must have been similiar to the medieval ones that are conserved in the *takas* or *alhanías* at the ends of the north gallery. They are an abstract image of light reflected on the water of the pool, much in the style of Braque in this century.

The south wall has a very recent ceramic dado copied from a sixteenth century one in the north gallery. This is a colonnade of seven arches covered by a seven-domed ceiling of "lazo" (strap-work). At the east and west ends are another two *takas,* the western one being a modern reconstruction and somewhat shallower than those in the north gallery. (Remember that the dimensions of this end are smaller than the other). The central arch of the gallery is higher than the others and rest on two capitals of *Mocarabes* in the style of Ispahan. Three others on each side are supported by cubic capitals.

Of the two doors which once existed on each side of the south wall only the one in the east corner with its plaster arch still stands, and leads by some stairs to the upper floor. The door at the other side used to lead to some rooms which disappeared when the Palace of Charles V was built, like the door itself.

Behind the central arch is the so-called "crypt of the Emperor's Palace". It is reached through the remains of a room severed diagonally by the stones of the renaissance palace. This room was similiar in its shape and size to the *Sala de la Barca,* although not so high. It probably lead to the vanished *Sala de las Helias* which, together with the *Corredor de las Helias* must have formed a building of generous proportions, since the time taken in its demolition and the number of labourers hired alone (15 to 30) suggest that it was indeed a considerable structure. Within this complex was to be found the gateway, now moved to the Court of the Mexuar, and the corridor to the Court of Lions.

The intrados of the arch which leads to the crypt —of which we will write later— is adorned with foliate decoration in delicate tones of blue and above the arch are three windows with plaster jalousies. Above the roof of this gallery there is a long room which has seven windows opening onto the court (the central one, an *Ajimez*) and all have modern wooden jalousies. This long room which connects with the upper part of the Court of Lions was a concession to the women of the household, a form of discreet observation gallery from where they could watch the goings-on in the court without being seen.

There is a third floor above this last room. This is a seven arched gallery with a lazo ceiling. The central arch has a straight lintel, higher than the others and resting on decorated hammer beams. All the voids of this upper gallery are closed off by wooden jalousies in the form of a parapet and which were made in the last century...

The plaster inscriptions of the southern portico are principally praises to God with a few dedicated to the Sultan. They are mostly copies of those at the north end.

Each of the buildings on the long sides of the court has five doors. On the west side the first door (south end) was used as the main entrance to the court for a long time, and the last door on this side (north end), next to the present entrance, communicates with the upper floor via a staircase where the Hispano-Musulman Museum is situated. The first door on the east side (at the southern end) has connected since the Christian occupation with the Court of Lions and with the eastern doorway of the Palace of Charles V. The last door on the east side (northen end by the gallery) was the original entrance to the Baths of Comares. All these edifices, for which the exact functions are not known, have two floors. The upper ones are lit from balconies with ajimez windows. The presence of platforms made of brick on the floors of some of the rooms has lead to them being written about as the women's quarters. However the civil servants of the time worked sitting on low daises, and the women lived in the Court of Lions.

The North Gallery has great similarities with the southern one because many of the decorative elements and epigraphs are copied from the northern one, which we shall now describe.

It has the same number of arches and the same layout of supporting members on capitals. The large central arch rests on Isphahan type capitals and the rest on cubic ones. Above the dado of sixteenth century tiles there is a poem by *Ibn Zamrak*, written in Hispano-Cursive characters. In one of the verses it says, *"You have conquered Algeciras by the strength of the sword, you opened an unknown door to our victory"*.

The ceiling of this gallery together with part of the *Sala de la Barca* (Hall of the Boat) was destroyed in the fire of 1890 and masterfully rebuilt later re-using many of the surviving burnt pieces.

LA SALA DE LA BARCA

The greeting *Baraka* (a blessing) appears everywhere. It was the repetition of this word in the Sala de la Barca which seems to be responsible for its name by corrupting the phonetics. Considering also the similarity between the ceiling and a upturned boat, "barca" in Spanish, the name is all the more justified.

To many it may seem strange, rather modern, that the Sala de la Barca was the winter throne room. In Assyriam reliefs we see the king lying on a dais surrounded by servants offering him wine and fruits. This room has two alcoves, one at each end, each with a Saracen arch. The western one has a toilet. In the cold winters of Granada the Sultan received people lying down as the Hall of Ambassadors was too large and cold to be comfortable.

In the jambs of the entrance arch there are some finely sculptured marble niches which were used to hold jars of water, perfumes or flowers. Almost always water was a symbol of hospitality, as one gathers from the translation of the poem about the niches.

The cold-coloured ceramics of the dado date this construction to the first half of the fourteenth century. The ceiling a semicylindrical vault, was destroyed in the fire of 1890 but the present one which was built in 1965 compares favourably with the original.

The direct entrance to the Hall of the Ambassadors is under a large arch. Beyond this there are two narrow spaces. The left-hand one has a small door through which one can reach the different floors of the tower —these stairs offer a wide variety of vaulting on each landing and the right-hand one is a small oratory where the *Mihrab* has been turned into a window giving light from the Patio de Lindaraja.

In the jambs of the next arch are two more small niches with verses in finely worked plaster giving clear reference to the water they contained, as on the right-hand one where it says, *"The jar of water within me is like the faithful one in the quibla of the temple who remains absorbed in God... giving relief to those who thirst"*. In the left-hand one it says, *"Whosoever comes to me thirsting I will lead him to a place where he will find clean water, cool, sweet and unpolluted"*.

One can still see the remains of the gold leaf in the hollows of the *mocarabes* of this arch, and in the niches or *takas* are the remnants of the polychroming.

The large slabs of marble that are to be found on the jambs of the entrance arches below the niches were also painted with blue and gold and sometimes decorated with stylized deer of the type on the jar exhibited in the Hispano-Musulman Museum. One of these polychromed jambs, originally from the Alhambra and in good condition, is in the National Archeological Museum, Madrid.

THE HALL OF THE AMBASSADORS: Remains magnificent even stripped of its stained glass windows which were lost in the explosion of 1590. This stained glass was a continuation of the design in ceramics on the dado, with the same geometry, where the fine lines interlaced in the ceramics were repeated in the lead fillets which held the coloured glass. The daylight was tinted by these colours and was cast onto the blue and gold floor tiles of which a few remain in the centre of the room, fenced off by chains. Not all the tiles thus protected are original. The few that are, are the ones where the blue glaze and the royal shields they surround are smooth, not with raised edges between the colours to hurt the feet as in the more modern copies made after the reconquest and amongst which the originals are dispersed.

This room is a square of 11.30 metres each side, with three openings 2.50 metres deep on each side —this being the thickness of the walls of the tower— the centre window being and ajimez and the ceilings fine wooden "artesonados". The windows, which open to the north, east and west have two small windows above each. Almost at the cornice which supports the splendid ceiling there are five windows on all four sides which are reminiscent of desert architecture. Those on the south side have been filled in as a means of reinforcing the wall against collapse.

La Alcazaba — The Fortress — Citadelle — Die Festung — Rocca fortificata

Albaycín

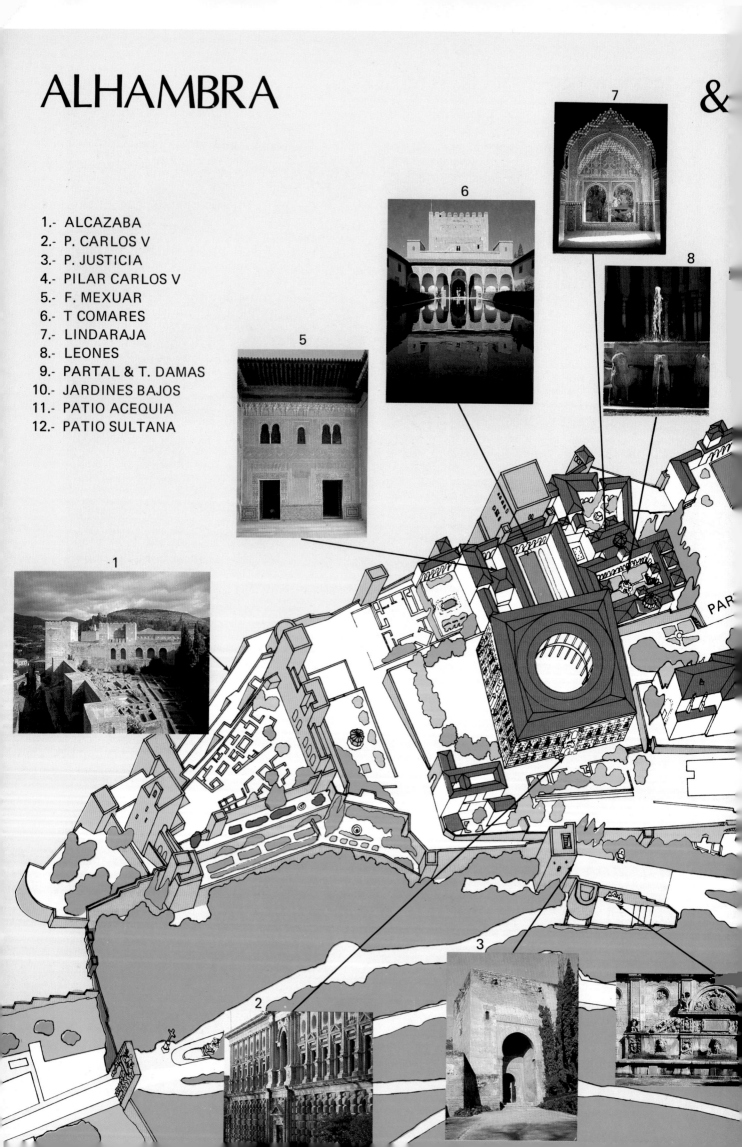

ALHAMBRA &

1.- ALCAZABA
2.- P. CARLOS V
3.- P. JUSTICIA
4.- PILAR CARLOS V
5.- F. MEXUAR
6.- T COMARES
7.- LINDARAJA
8.- LEONES
9.- PARTAL & T. DAMAS
10.- JARDINES BAJOS
11.- PATIO ACEQUIA
12.- PATIO SULTANA

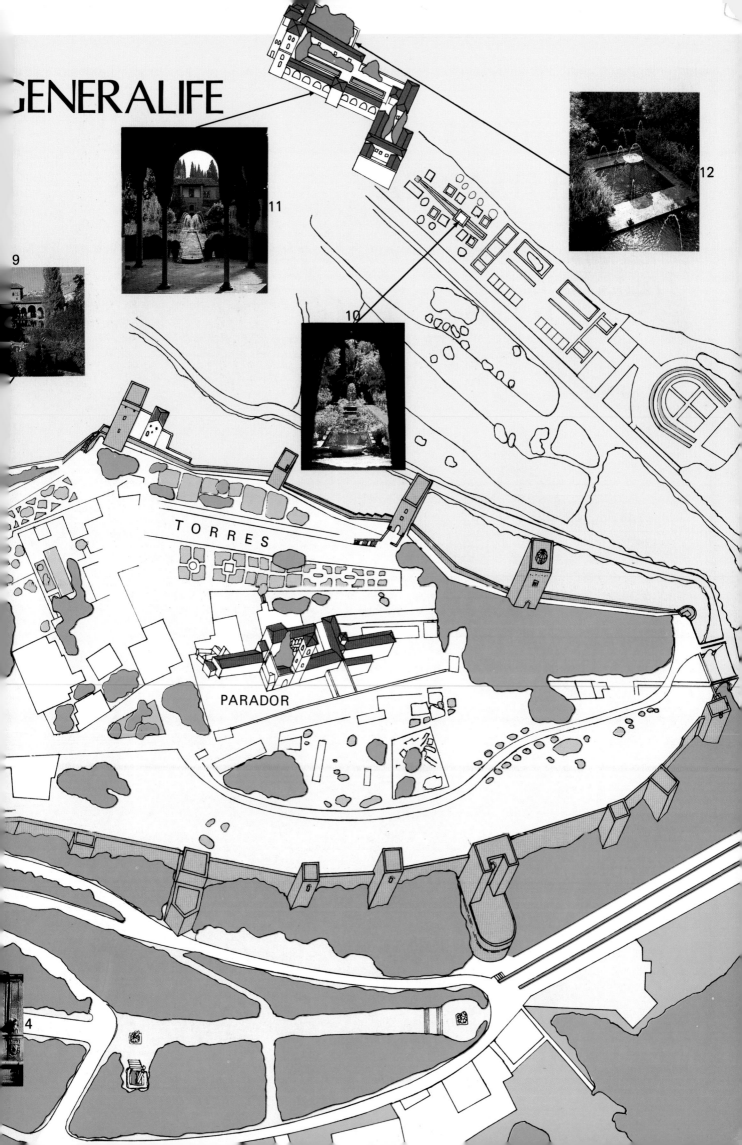

GENERALIFE

9

11

12

10

TORRES

PARADOR

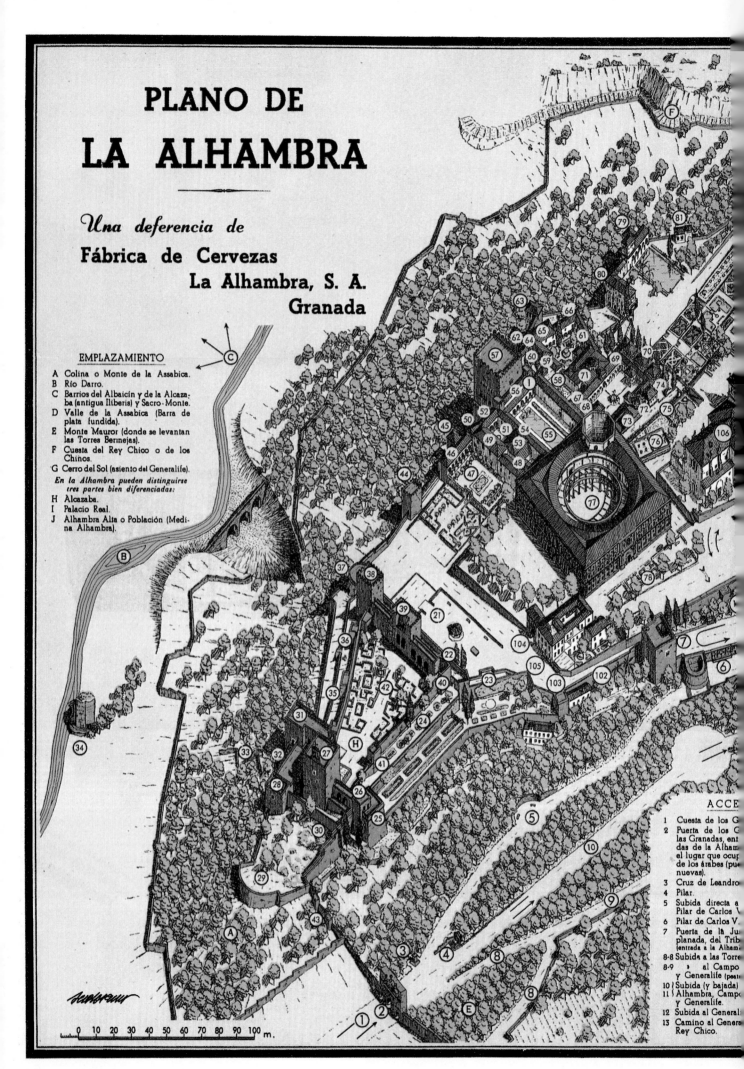

PLANO DE LA ALHAMBRA

Una deferencia de
**Fábrica de Cervezas
La Alhambra, S. A.
Granada**

EMPLAZAMIENTO

A Colina o Monte de la Assabica.
B Río Darro.
C Barrios del Albaicín y de la Alcazaba (antigua Iliberis) y Sacro-Monte.
D Valle de la Assabica (Barra de plata fundida).
E Monte Mauror (donde se levantan las Torres Bermejas).
F Cuesta del Rey Chico o de los Chinos.
G Cerro del Sol (asiento del Generalife).

En la Alhambra pueden distinguirse tres partes bien diferenciadas:

H Alcazaba.
I Palacio Real.
J Alhambra Alta o Población (Medina Alhambra).

0 10 20 30 40 50 60 70 80 90 100 m.

DOCUMENTACION TECNICA: Planos y maqueta de la Escuela de Arquitectura de Madrid.

ACCE

1 Cuesta de los G
2 Puerta de los G las Granadas, ent das de la Alham el lugar que ocup de los árabes (pu nuevas).
3 Cruz de Leandro
4 Pilar.
5 Subida directa a Pilar de Carlos V
6 Pilar de Carlos V.
7 Puerta de la Ju planada, del Trib (entrada a la Alham
8-8 Subida a las Torre
8-9 » al Campo y Generalife (pea
10 Subida (y bajada)
11 Alhambra, Campo y Generalife.
12 Subida al General
13 Camino al Genera Rey Chico.

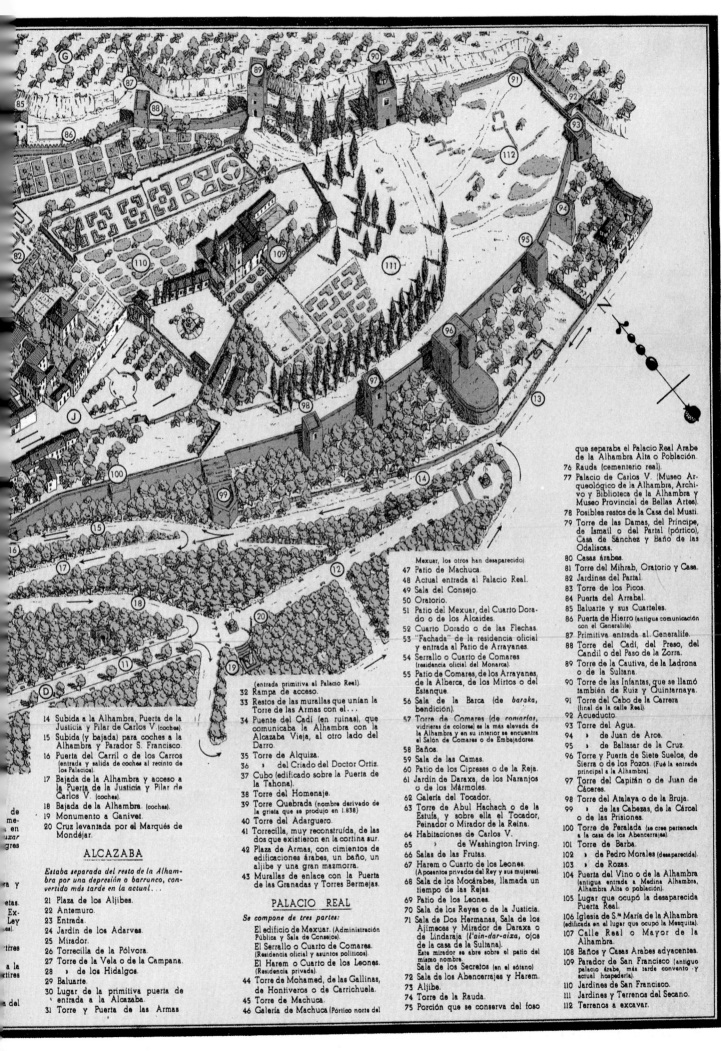

que separaba el Palacio Real Árabe de la Alhambra Alta o Población.
76 Rauda (cementerio real).
77 Palacio de Carlos V. (Museo Arqueológico de la Alhambra, Archivo y Biblioteca de la Alhambra y Museo Provincial de Bellas Artes).
78 Posibles restos de la Casa del Musti
79 Torre de las Damas, del Príncipe, de Ismail o del Partal (pórtico), Casa de Sánchez y Baño de las Odaliscas.
80 Casas árabes.
81 Torre del Mihrab, Oratorio y Casa.
82 Jardines del Partal.
83 Torre de los Picos.
84 Puerta del Arrabal.
85 Baluarte y sus Cuarteles.
86 Puerta de Hierro (antigua comunicación con el Generalife).
87 Primitiva entrada al Generalife.
88 Torre del Cadí, del Preso, del Candil o del Paso de la Zorra.
89 Torre de la Cautiva, de la Ladrona o de la Sultana.
90 Torre de las Infantas, que se llamó también de Ruiz y Quintarnaya.
91 Torre del Cabo de la Carrera (final de la calle Real).
92 Acueducto.
93 Torre del Agua.
94 » de Juan de Arce.
95 » de Baltasar de la Cruz.
96 Torre y Puerta de Siete Suelos, de Sierra o de los Pozos. (Fué la entrada principal a la Alhambra).
97 Torre del Capitán o de Juan de Cáceres.
98 Torre del Atalaya o de la Bruja.
99 » de las Cabezas, de la Cárcel o de las Prisiones.
100 Torre de Peralada (se cree pertenecía a la casa de los Abencerrajes).
101 Torre de Barba.
102 » de Pedro Morales (desaparecida).
103 » de Rozas.
104 Puerta del Vino o de la Alhambra (antigua entrada a Medina Alhambra, Alhambra Alta o población).
105 Lugar que ocupó la desaparecida Puerta Real.
106 Iglesia de S.ª María de la Alhambra (edificada en el lugar que ocupó la Mezquita).
107 Calle Real o Mayor de la Alhambra.
108 Baños y Casas Árabes adyacentes.
109 Parador de San Francisco (antiguo palacio árabe, más tarde convento y actual hospedería).
110 Jardines de San Francisco.
111 Jardines y Terrenos del Secano.
112 Terrenos a excavar.

Mexuar, los otros han desaparecido).
47 Patio de Machuca.
48 Actual entrada al Palacio Real.
49 Sala del Consejo.
50 Oratorio.
51 Patio del Mexuar, del Cuarto Dorado o de los Alcaides.
52 Cuarto Dorado o de las Flechas.
53 "Fachada" de la residencia oficial y entrada al Patio de Arrayanes.
54 Serrallo o Cuarto de Comares (residencia oficial del Monarca).
55 Patio de Comares, de los Arrayanes, de la Alberca, de los Mirtos o del Estanque.
56 Sala de la Barca (de *baraka*, bendición).
57 Torre de Comares (de *comarías*, vidrieras de colores) es la más elevada de la Alhambra y en su interior se encuentra el Salón de Comares o de Embajadores.
58 Baños.
59 Sala de las Camas.
60 Patio de los Cipreses o de la Reja.
61 Jardín de Daraxa, de los Naranjos o de los Mármoles.
62 Galería del Tocador.
63 Torre de Abul Hachach o de la Estufa, y sobre ella el Tocador, Peinador o Mirador de la Reina.
64 Habitaciones de Carlos V.
65 » de Washington Irving.
66 Salas de las Frutas.
67 Harem o Cuarto de los Leones. (Aposentos privados del Rey y sus mujeres).
68 Sala de los Mocárabes, llamada un tiempo de las Rejas.
69 Patio de los Leones.
70 Sala de los Reyes o de la Justicia.
71 Sala de Dos Hermanas, Sala de los Ajimeces y Mirador de Daraxa o de Lindaraja (*l'ain-dar-aixa*, ojos de la casa de la Sultana). Este mirador se abre sobre el patio del mismo nombre.
Sala de los Secretos (en el sótano)
72 Sala de los Abencerrajes y Harem.
73 Aljibe.
74 Torre de la Rauda.
75 Porción que se conserva del foso

(entrada primitiva al Palacio Real).
32 Rampa de acceso.
33 Restos de las murallas que unían la Torre de las Armas con el...
34 Puente del Cadí (en ruinas), que comunicaba la Alhambra con la Alcazaba Vieja, al otro lado del Darro.
35 Torre de Alquiza.
36 » del Criado del Doctor Ortiz.
37 Cubo (edificado sobre la Puerta de la Tahona).
38 Torre del Homenaje.
39 Torre Quebrada (nombre derivado de la grieta que se produjo en 1.838)
40 Torre del Adarguero.
41 Torrecilla, muy reconstruída, de las dos que existieron en la cortina sur.
42 Plaza de Armas, con cimientos de edificaciones árabes, un baño, un aljibe y una gran mazmorra.
43 Murallas de enlace con la Puerta de las Granadas y Torres Bermejas.

PALACIO REAL

Se compone de tres partes:
El edificio de Mexuar. (Administración Pública y Sala de Consejo).
El Serrallo o Cuarto de Comares. (Residencia oficial y asuntos políticos).
El Harem o Cuarto de los Leones. (Residencia privada).
44 Torre de Mohamed, de las Gallinas, de Hontiveros o de Carrichuela.
45 Torre de Machuca.
46 Galería de Machuca (Pórtico norte del

14 Subida a la Alhambra, Puerta de la Justicia y Pilar de Carlos V. (coches).
15 Subida (y bajada) para coches a la Alhambra y Parador S. Francisco.
16 Puerta del Carril o de los Carros (entrada y salida de coches al recinto de los Palacios).
17 Bajada de la Alhambra y acceso a la Puerta de la Justicia y Pilar de Carlos V. (coches).
18 Bajada de la Alhambra. (coches).
19 Monumento a Ganivet.
20 Cruz levantada por el Marqués de Mondéjar.

ALCAZABA

Estaba separada del resto de la Alhambra por una depresión o barranco, convertido más tarde en la actual...
21 Plaza de los Aljibes.
22 Antemuro.
23 Entrada.
24 Jardín de los Adarves.
25 Mirador.
26 Torrecilla de la Pólvora.
27 Torre de la Vela o de la Campana.
28 » de los Hidalgos.
29 Baluarte.
30 Lugar de la primitiva puerta de entrada a la Alcazaba.
31 Torre y Puerta de las Armas

Bosque de la Alhambra — The forest — Le bois — Der Wald — Il bosco

Puerta del vino — The Gate of wine — La porte du vin — Weintor — Porta del vino

Oratorio y Albaycín — View on the Albaycín — Vue sur l'Albaycin — Aussicht über den Albaycin — Moschea e l'Albaycin

Mexuar

Fachada de Comares — Façade of comares — Façade de Comares — Hauptfassade von Comares

Patio de los Arrayanes —

Salón del trono — Hall of the ambassadors — Salon du trone — Thronsaal — Salone del trono

The central window ledge on the north side was the throne, according to the inscriptions on the wall above the tiling in this area where it says, "(...) *Yusuf* (...) *chose me to be the seat of the kingdom. The lord of this kingdom makes it a great and divine throne".* From this position the Sultan exercised a certain psychological hold over the citizens of the capital who at the same time would have felt themselves under the gaze of the religious political and military head of the kingdom. From the moment they entered the doorway of the Sala de la Barca, the ambassadors would have felt intimidated by the silhouette of the Sultan seated against the light of the stained glass and looking upon them as they advanced across a sumptuous scenario of brilliant colours and sparkling gold.

Before the southern windows were filled in, the Sultan would have been able to sit or lie on his throne and simultaneously enjoy the view of the city with its gardens, and the reflections of the windows and sky on the water which lay before his eyes in the Court of Myrtles.

The ceiling is the masterpiece of the carpenters of the kingdom. It rests on a cornice of painted wooden "mocarabes" where one can read the *Sura LXVII* of the Koran or the Kingdom. In the third *Aleya* it says, *"He did make seven heavens one above the other; no discord will you see in this pious creation".* This is a clear reference to the seven heavens spoken of in the Koran in three of its *suras (II-27, LXVII-3 & LXXVIII-12),* surely referring to the design on the ceiling of the room. This is made up of 8,017 pieces of wood with superimposed reliefs in cedar and made into various symmetrical panels

framed in a boss of mocarabes at the top of the dome. Don Darío Cabanelas found a plaque showing the colours to be applied to this ceiling, white, red, walnut-white, light green, red, green and once again red in that order.

According to *Ibn Abass* the "Sevens Heavens" were made as follows: the first of emeralds, the second of red marigolds, the third of red hyacinths, the fourth of the whitest silver, the fifth of gold, the sixth of pearl and the seventh of brilliant light.

From this description of the seven heavens comes the legend *"mi' ray"* of the voyage of the Prophet to heaven mounted on a white horse in the company of the angel Gabriel and described in "The Ascent of Mahoma" by *Ibn Arabi* from Murcia. Don Miguel Asín Palacios finds it has much in common with Dante's "Divine Comedy". Indeed Dante's teacher, Bruneto Latini, was at the School of Translators in Toledo when King Alfonso X commissioned the translation of the Murcian *sufi* into Latin, and it's quite possible that Dante Alighieri got hold of a copy of "The Ascent of Mahoma" through him and used it as a model for the "Divine Comedy".

Amongst all the cufic, magrebie and hispano-cursive characters which include religious themes, the constant repetition of the device "Only God is the Victor" and the praises to Yusuf I (and one must be impressed by the decorative value of the Arabic epigraphy) and just visible on the capital of one of the niche arches, is a text indicating the public nature of the hall. Begging brevity, it says,

"Few words and you will leave in peace"

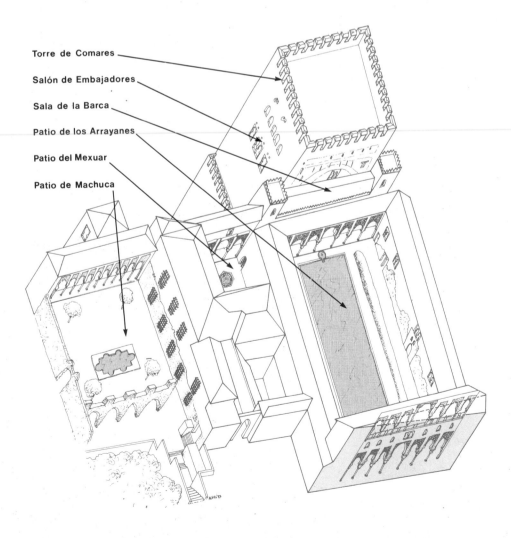

Torre de Comares

Salón de Embajadores

Sala de la Barca

Patio de los Arrayanes

Patio del Mexuar

Patio de Machuca

THE COURT OF LIONS

This was the centre of the Sultan's household and included the area given to the women of the royal house. It cannot be called harem for its function was not exclusively feminine in nature, as it was also used for activities related to diplomatic and political life of the kingdom.

Its proportions are those of a rectangle of 28.55 by 16.00 metres, excluding the narrow marble pavements added recently around the 124 columns. However, in the outer rectangle formed by the walls of the surrounding buildings, we can see a clear irregularity. The east wall (20.22 metres) is wider by 0.42 metres than the wall of the Hall of the Mocarabes (19.80 metres). This difference of nearly half a metre could be the result of a necessary change in line towards a building on the south side which probably existed at the time when Muhammad V commenced the construction of the court. This was a rational solution and exactly the opposite of what Machuca did with the Emperor's Palace, when he "forced" the south-west angle in the gallery of the Court of Myrtles.

We known now that on the 30th December 1362 the Court of Lions consisted of no more than the Hall of the Two Sister and the buildings that now enclose it were erected after this date. The entrance was through a small door in the southern corner of the court and it leads into a small lobby which still contains remains of fine foliate decoration and benches for the guards. On the right-hand side of this lobby there a great door can still be seen which must have connected with the *Hall of Helias* or *Elias*. This no longer exists but Emilio García Gómez suggests that the name could be a mistranslation caused by the omission of some diacritical sign or some vowel in the Arabic word *"al-'inas",* meaning "friendly reception". It would fit the function of the missing hall perfectly.

As you passed through the entrance to the Court of Lions, its beauty unfolded again little by whichever of the two paths the colonnaded cloister directed you. A forest of golden columns opened up before the visitor and, continuing slowly along, resembled *"the golden fringes of a spread of lace suspended from the sky"*, because the garden plants in the middle prevented you from seeing how the pillars rested on their marble bases.

The uniformity of capitals and arches is only illusory since there is great decorative diversity which is not apparent at first. The shafts of the columns are joined to the bases and capitals by lead joints so that reasonable thermal movement can be accommodated and a perfect assembly could be achieved for the three elements.

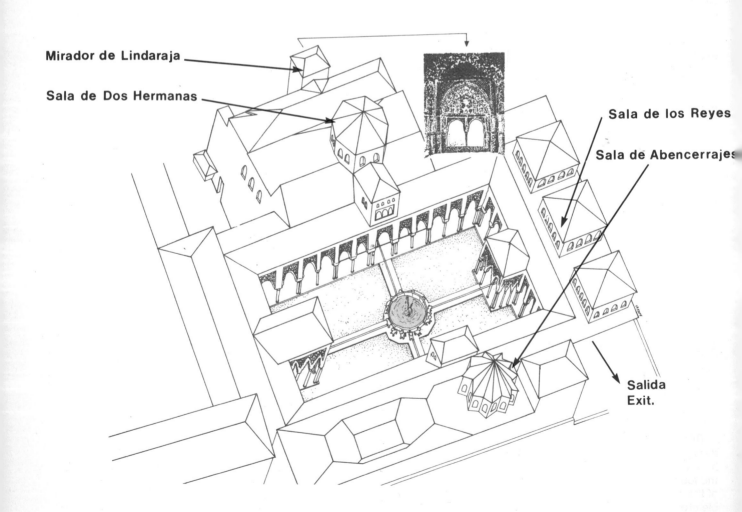

Mirador de Lindaraja

Sala de Dos Hermanas

Sala de los Reyes

Sala de Abencerrajes

Salida
Exit.

PATIO DE LOS LEONES

The shorter two sides of the court are not symmetrical either. On the east side on each flank of the prominent pavilion the columns stand in two pairs and a single one, whereas on the opposite side are two single columns and one pair on each flank.

On the east and west sides of the court are two pavilions which intrude into the quadrilateral, each with a small fountain. The coffered ceilings of these pavilions are beautiful wooden domes which still conserve some of the original polychroming. These are two perfect hemispheres made with flat components. The western pavilion has its roof built above the original cornice and the intervening space is decorated with imperial eagles in plaster, recalling the period when its height was altered. This change in height is not entirely capricious as we shall see later, but a consequence of the difference in the line of sight between a man seated on the floor or lying down and another man standing up. The eastern pavilion had a glazed ceramic dome for many years, the result of the Byzantinism associated with the Arab period in the Romantic era, and fortunately removed in 1934, thus removing too an excessive weight from the structure of the pavilion.

In the centre of the court the *Fountain of the Lions* sprays water and refreshes the atmosphere through the mouths of twelve white marble lions, which as they stand in a circle watch over every nook and cranny of the court. On their backs they carry a dodecagonal (twelve-sided) bowl and on its sides one can read a *qasida* by Ibn Zamrak which apart of being beautiful, explains many of the details of the court and of the fountain. Are these the same gilded copper lions which Ibn Aljatib saw before the court was built? If don Emilio García Gómez does not dare to declare that these could be the same stone lions, once painted copper gilt, then neither are we going to make this affirmation. The theory nevertheless exists that the lions were once polychromed and there is evidence that they have been scraped.

The bowl rested on the backs of the lions and it was restored there in 1966 as we can see it now, having removed the plinths which formerly raised it to a more "Christian" level. The cylinder of marble which carries the spout, formed by perforating the top, has two rows of eight holes superimposed in it. The larger holes are in the lower row, so that the water entered via the smaller upper holes and exited by the larger ones, preserving a still surface on the water in which the sky was reflected. This reflection is perhaps referred to in a verse of the poem:

> Is it not in truth that white cloud which pours its streams
> upon the lions and seems as the hand of the Calif, who
> every morning casts his favours to the lions of war?.

Basing his theory on a beautiful poem by the Jew Ibn Gabirol, Frederick P. Bargebour in his book "The Alhambra Palace of the Eleventh Century" maintains that the lions came from a fountain in the palace of Samuel Ibn Agrella where the Palace Hotel now stands and that its original dodecahedral bowl is set in the floor of the Hall of the Abencerrajes. On two recent occasions this bowl has been lifted out without finding any signs of seatings on its base. It is generally believed that these lions date from the end of the tenth century or early eleventh century.

This court with its arches of perforated tracery forming rhombuses and its colonnades of fine pillars seems inspired by the Cistercian cloisters of the period, a theory aided by the fountain in the centre of the court. The rooms at the sides of the court are joined to the Lions Fountain by a sort of marble cross. Along its canals the water flows from the fountains to the halls of Abencerrajes and the Two Sisters and from the centre of the two pavilions.

THE HALL OF THE MOCARABES: This is the first room as one enters from the Court of Myrtles and the nearest to the original entrance. The name *mocárabes* means kinds of prefabricated plaster pieces which made up the vaulting. Wrecked in the explosion of 1590 this was replaced by a baroque ceiling of plaster. In the last century the southern end of the vault was taken down revealing the remains of the original, where one can see some of the polychroming and the spring of earlier work.

THE HALL OF THE ABENCERRAJES: We find this to the right as we pass anti clockwise through the colonnade. It is said that in Granada myth and history are so intermixed that at times it is difficult to determine where one begins and the other ends. The name *Abencerrajes* belongs to a family of Granada of great political importance. Their rivals, the Zenetes, formed a conspiracy which implicated the Sultana in an amorous adventure, thus exciting the jealousy of the Sultan and leading to the massacre of thirty-six Abencerraje knights in this very hall, on the occasion of a party. This legend which was to inspire "The Last Abencerraje" by Chateaubriand, occured during the reigns of a number of kings of Granada. Popular opinion has it that the red marks —iron oxide— on the bottom of the pool are the blood of the murdered knights.

This dodecagonal fountain is the central piece of the room. When filled and calm it reflects the magnificent mocárabes of the ceiling, with and eight-pointed star in the vaulting. From a seated position behind the fountain, before the Lions Fountain had the present spout, the view was a series of brilliant reflective planes and, at the far end through the Mirador of Lindaraja in the Hall of the Two Sisters one could see the old city and the sky. The original tiles in this room were taken to the Alcazar of Seville and replaced by the present ones in the sixteenth century.

At the exit from this room there are two passageways: the left-had one leads to the afore-mentioned vestibule which leads to the Hall of the Helias and links with the original entrance, passing first an undecorated room which some describe as a water-cistern. The presence here of a window which once was a door opening into the *Rawda* or royal burial ground could reinforce the hypothesis that the supposed cistern was some kind of prison where political enemies were executed in secret and buried at night in the adjoining cemetery. Popular rumours of this kind were probably the source of the legend of the Abencerraje killings.

The other passage leads to a stairway to the upper floor. This was probably where the women and younger children lived. At the same level we find the *Hall of the Yanan* with the remains of painted dados and black marble cornices.

In the south-east corner of the court is another exit leading to the gardens of the Partal and passing through a shell-domed tower. This is obviously another entrance to the Court of Lions coming from the Arrabal Gate near the Torre de los Picos which communicated with the approach road to the Generalife.

THE HALL OF KINGS: This occupies the whole east end of the Court of Lions. It is divided into five spaces; three of them lit by the access porticoes and separated by another two in the shade. In the springs of the vaulting of mocarabes there are twenty windows with plaster lattices. At the extreme ends are two alcoves with arches aligned along the axis of the room. From the southern alcove the rooms appear as a succession of areas of light and shade framed by plaster arches each different from the other. This variety of decoration and alternating lights and shades results in this heavy decoration being pleasant to the eye without tiring in the way baroque decorative elements do when repeated over and again. "The sensation of harmony with different elements" is achieved in the ideal formula of modern decorators.

In each of the illuminated areas there are alcoves but those who have written about this room cannot agree about their use in olden times. At the risk of being accused of fantasising, the author of this work surmises that the Hall of Kings was the "Great Hall" of the house, where each alcove was a reserved space for the different groups of family or political factions. Along this hall the spectacle was presented and the artists, dancers, jugglers, conjurers and jesters went along repeating their turn in front of each group. In this way the guests did not have to move about and the alcoves at the ends would have housed the orchestras.

Between each alcove and in each end one there are small lobbies. Their use tends to be glossed over in the descriptions of the Hall of Kings. Those alcoves at the end were the stairs to an upper gallery behind the Court of Lions. This was later transformed becoming the *Casa de doña Clara,* which was demolished in 1885. By this time the doors and stairs had long since disappeared. The other two were used for storing files at the time of the Catholic Monarchs, stripping them of any sign of their original use. From this same period date the yoke and arrows and the motto "Tanto Monta", which can be seen over the first arch on the south side and which marks the site of the altar of the first church of Santa María.

On the ceilings of the bigger alcoves there are paintings on vellum fixed to their wooden backing with paste and tiny bamboo pegs. This fixing system avoided damage which the rusting of iron nails would produce, and at the same time prevented the paintings from falling as the nails fixed in the wood loosened because of the differential thermal movement of the materials.

Veritable rivers of ink have been spent about the meaning of these paintings. Nowadays, however, there is little opposition to the demonstrated assertion of the French arabist Massignon.He destroyed the false argument which denies the eastern origin of these paintings founded on a supposed Koranic prohibition of representing living beings, the paintings of the Kings Hall are Moslem, even if influenced by western models, and it is generally believed that they were made in the late fourteenth or early fifteenth century. In fact in the Sura V, Aleya 92, the sacred book of the Mohammedans says:

> "Oh, all those who believe! Verily, wine and the anzab, and the maisir and arrows (are) abominations and works by Shaitan; avoid them and probably you would be happy".

Thus all that is forbidden in relation to living beings are the *anzab* or idols which can be objects of adoration. This limitation is not exclusive to Islam; worshipping of idols is also prohibited in the Old Testament and in the Talmud. The false prohibition could have been inspired by one of the *hadices* composed after the Prophet's death. Out of the ninety four *hadices* which are known, only four of them are definitely contemporary with the Prophet, all the rest being considered apocryphal. Also there are so many examples of living beings in Islamic art that just counting them would give the lie to this pretended prohibition.

The central alcove, given its privileged position, would have housed the Sultan and his intimates. Seated within, the perspective is of an oasis seen through a forest of palm trees with the Fountain of Lions at its centre. There exists a drawing in the book "Granada" by Prieto Moreno of this inspired example of natural architecture.

On the ceiling of this alcove ten persons are also painted who are traditionally thought to be the first ten kings of the dynasty. It is also generally accepted that these paintings represent all the kings from Muhammad I up to Muhammad

V —the builder of this palace— but then two kings are missing. However one must remember that the latter had two usurpers during his reign and it is quite natural that neither he nor his immediate successors would include these adventurers as monarchs.

The silhouettes of hands and faces and the stars which divide the composition horizontally into two halves are painted on a golden background, all being reminiscent of early Byzantine panels. In these paintings one can see two large armorials (a bend of gold on a field of gules swallowed by two dragons) showing the coat of arms of the dynasty. In a form of fringe to the concave oval which forms this ceiling, one can see nineteen small shields of the same colour and metal but without the dragons.

The paintings in the other two alcoves share certain thematic elements. Two personages, one Christian and one Moslem, to judge by their arms and dress, perform a series of tests and trials, apparently for the favour of a Christian lady. All this terminates in the next alcove where the Moslem defeats his rival with a lance thrust before the pleading Christian dame who watches the trial from a tower. Filled with abundant iconography, the style of these last two paintings is almost early Tuscan.

THE HALL OF THE TWO SISTER: Contrary to earlier opinion and as a consequence of the latest book by Emilio García Gómez this is now recognised as the oldest of the rooms around the Court of Lions.

As with all the other adjuncts of this court where we do not know the original name, the one given is merely descriptive. It is called The Two Sisters because of the two large Macael marble slabs in the centre of the room.

This room was used as the Hall of the Ambassadors by Muhammad V and replaced that built by this father for the same purpose in the Tower of Comares. It is decorated with a tiled dado decorated with the family coat of arms and metallic glazes, perhaps the most unusual in the whole of the Alhambra. Above this dado, written in Spanish cursive characters, is a beautiful *qasida* by Ibn Zamrak which covers the four walls. Starting from the left (facing the Fountain of the Lions) it describes the beauty of the room, comparing it to a beautiful garden. It also speaks of the marvellous vault of mocarabes which cover the room, a real masterpiece of over four thousand pieces.

The square floor of the eight-by-eight-metres room changes to an octagon in the upper part by means of squinches of mocarabes which support the eight-sided ceiling. Two windows are placed in each plane of the octagon and until 1590 they projected coloured light through stained glass. The aesthetic effect of the room is captured in a verse of the afore-mentioned *qasida,* in which it says: *"... in this the soul will find a beauteous dream".*

Curiously this poem mentions the "Five Pleiades", when in fact this group of stars in the constellation of Taurus can be seen to be six in number and even seven. In this particular case the "stars" are Adam and Abraham; stars of the natural law; Moses, star of the law of scripture; Jesus, star of the law of grace and Mohammed, star of the koranic law.

Entering this hall from the Court of Lions we can see two narrow passages to left and right, as in the Hall of the Abencerrajes. The right-hand one provides stairs to the first floor and the left gives access to a toilet.

The Hall of the Two Sister is paved with great slabs of marble and at each side of a small fountain there are the two largest ones which give the room its name. Crossing the room we see at the end of it the *Mirador de Lindaraja.*

Perhaps because of some confusion over a reference by the Baron de Shack to a water fountain which existed in Toledo, in a certain guide book for Morrocans, the Fountain of

Lions is described as a water clock, a fact which is patently untrue. However all the Alhambra is a sundial. At the equinox, a ray of sun projects the reflection of the north canal (remember the white marble cross with the Fountain of Lions in the centre) exactly on the vertical centrum of the arch of the Hall of the Ajimeces. One can follow the passage of the hours by the movement of this ray of the sun exactly as if it were the shadow cast by the gnomon of a sundial.

Passing through the Hall of the Ajimeces with its windows to left and right and with a ceiling of mocarabes we find ourselves in the fabulous **MIRADOR OF LINDARAJA.** The name seems to be derived from the Arabic *"ain-dar-Aixa"* (the eye of Aixa's House). It is possible that once he had finished the Court of the Lions and what remained to be done of the Court of Myrtles, Muhammad V once again used the Hall of Ambassadors and designated the Hall of the Two Sisters for use by the Sultana (*dar-al-Malika*) and the royal family as a residence. This arrangement is described by Hernando de Baeza, former interpreter to the court of Boabdil and then secretary of the Catholic Monarchs. This gazebo, with window ledges at the original height, has on its north side a beautiful "ajimez" which overlooks *the Garden of Lindaraja.*

Before the Christian gallery which encloses the garden was built one could see the city over the walls, and then turning towards the Court of Lions from a seated position on the floor one saw the sky through the window over the arch at the entrance to the Hall of the Two Sisters. Horizontally one saw the fountain of this room and the mirror of water of the Fountain of Lions. Crowning this gazebo which once housed the throne is a stained glass dome held in the finest of wooden tracery. This filled the room with multicoloured lights in olden times.

Around the ajimez of the gazebo is a poem from which we quote this fragment:

> *"Certainly I am within this garden, an eye filled with joy, and the very apple of my eye is my Lord".*

Could this poetic image of the eye have something to do with the provisional throne and the name of the gazebo?

All the dados here in are formed of very smallest tiles or cut ceramics and the jambs of the arch which separate the gazebo from the Hall of the Ajimeces have ceramic inscriptions in black which refer to Muhammad V; they are cursive Arabic script and seem to be inlaid in a white background.

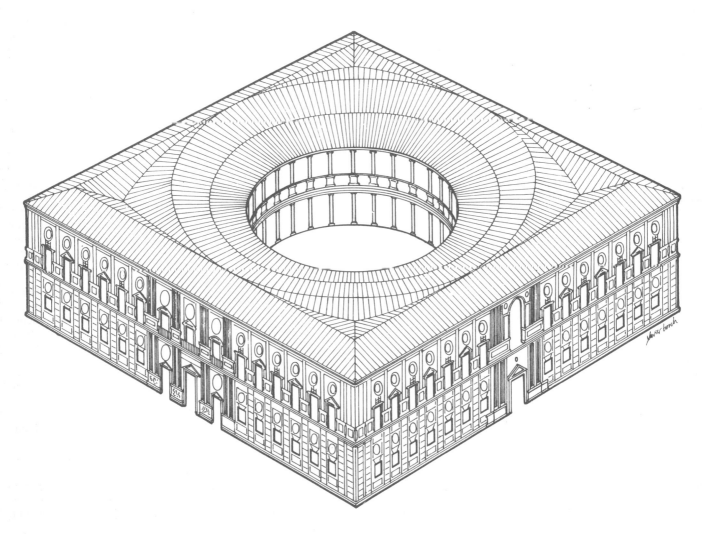

THE PALACE OF CHARLES V

n the history of art there can be no building more vilified than the palace commissioned by Charles V next to the Alhambra (the royal palace of the Mussulmanś).

It must be understood that, although he was unbeaten in his European campaigns and Paladin of the wars against Protestantism, Charles does not get a good press in European history and that all he did and all that he ordered built is mercilessly criticised. The many great things that were done in his reign go blindly and completely unrecognised.

Even worse, our own historians with a few exceptions have imbibed from these polluted sources which come from abroad. Thus we see, to show but one example, that don Francisco Pi Margall, without pausing to meditate on the architectural marvel he had before him, let his pen write, *"is this but a mass of stones distributed by neither intelligence nor sentiment, or is it simply the drafting of compass and rule?".*

Don Luis Hurtado de Mendoza had succeeded his father don Inigo when, in April 1562, he had news of the coming of the Emperor Charles V to Granada after his marriage to Isabel of Portugal in Seville that March. Bermúdez de Pedraza, the historian, tells us that the emperor did not intend to visit Granada, but did so at the request of certain personages and not solely because of the heat in Seville. They sang the praises of the city which thirty years earlier had been the pearl of the kingdom. Owing to its exotic past it was very attractive to the young king who had passed his early years in the monotony of the low countries.

On the twentieth of April the major-domo of the emperor arrived in Granada to organise the reception of his monarch, and finally on the fifth of June, Charles arrived in the company of the fair Isabel, one of the most beautiful women of her generation.

Seven years earlier an obscure reredos painter called *Pedro Machuca* had arrived, accompanying Jacobo Florentino el Indaco. They came from Italy where Machuca had spent some years —it is not known how many— frequenting Italian circles and, perhaps in the company of the Florentines, he came into contact with the leading figures of the *Arte Nuovo.* Its influence can be seen in the palace that was to immortalise him as an architect.

Despite *Antonio de Palomino* describing him as "a follower of Rafael", it seems that Machuca never reached the grade of Master Architect, and consequently his work was confined to the precincts of the Alhambra by special jurisdiction. He also counted on the patronage of *Luis Hurtado de Mendoza,* Count of Tendilla and Governor of the Alhambra, whom he had served as squire in 1526 and to whom he was probably bound by mutual affection. It is known that his oldest son and daughter were called Luisa and Luis in honour of his noble patron.

Once Charles and his followers had arrived in Granada they were installed in some rooms built the year before, next to the upper part of the *Baths of Comares* and around the *Court of Lindaraja* and had access to the rest of the palace through the *Hall of the Two Sisters* and the *Hall of Ambassadors.* The rooms later occupied by Washington Irving in 1829 were built for Isabel of Portugal, and an extra floor was added to the tower of *Abu-l-Haŷŷaŷ* which was to be known as the *"Peinador de la Reina".* The court was housed in different parts of the city and the Queen, after moving her lodgings to the warden's apartments above the Mexuar, decided finally to move to the Convent of the Jeronimas which had recently been built. Until December when the royal couple left the city,

this was the heart and brain of the Empire. By that time the empress was carrying the future Phillip II.

None of the more recent ancestors of Charles had had their own palace. With their ever-moving courts they lodged in the houses of the nobility, in castles or monasteries. Also since the reign of the Catholic Monarchs and the early years of Charles' reign the colonial expansion looked towards Africa and the new lands of America. In the geopolitics of those times Granada had a privileged position as an inland city but not too far from the ports of embarkation for these continents. Because of his European education Charles could not live in the Nasari Palace, so he decided to build a palace on the Red Hill.

Pedro Machuca was commissioned to carry out the work with funds that Queen* *Juana* of Castilla had destined, by order of her parents, for the repair of the old palaces, and 80,000 ducats which the emperor had received from the Moriscos of his kingdom. The Morisco rebellion of 1568 put an end to the regular income to finance the works. After the 1550s the emperor's interest in his palace in the Alhambra was on the wane. Also his succesor, Philip II who was crowned king in 1556, was more interested in building the Escorial, leaving the Palace in the Alhambra in a secondary position. Successive delays, almost always due to a lack of funds, resulted in an unfinished palace up to the present day. It is considered to be the first non-religious renaissance building in Spain.

On the four exterior frontages one can see great differences between the two floors. The lower floor with the characteristic *bugnato fiorentino* (rustication), conserves the robustness of a medieval castle, while on the first floor (direct first by* Luis Machuca and then by Juan de Orea) some "manerist" modifications by Juan de Herrera were introduced; for example, the illusion of walls of greater thickness produced by the round conical clerestory lights over the window.

On the western principal frontage the most notable features are the two winged, reclining women, softly carved in marble by the Flemish artist Antonio de Leval, which rest on the tympanum. He was also responsible for the cherubs above the tympana of the lateral doors, the medallions with Flemish warriors on them and the unfinished grey stone lions by the door of the south front. Earl E. Rosenthal attributes the right hand relief (which represents the Battle of Pavia and everybody is left-handed) to this same Leval, though it is probably by Pedro Machuca. The left-hand relief (right-handed people) is by Juan de Orea. All the other reliefs are allusions to the Triumph of Peace, with angels burning flags and the tools of war in the desire for disarmament.

The upper part of the facade is neither as rich nor as interesting. it gives the impression that the original design was simplified to the minimum possible. Here we truly see the "compass and ruler" which Pi y Margall spoke of. Two medallions by Ocampo of the trials of Hercules are the only sculptural features of note on this upper body of the facade.

The south front, on the other hand, has the two bodies of the facade in elegant harmony, although the reliefs by Nicolao di Corte do not have the strength of those on the main front. The other two fronts, to the north and east, lack any features of interest.

The thirty —metre diameter central court, reached by climbing a few steps, is the master work in this palace. The lower part of this monumental ring of thirty two Tuscan-Doric columns of a smooth pudding stone (porphyry), are remeniscent of Bramante's San Pietro in Montorio, as if it were cast from the same mould as that building but in negative and on a much larger scale. The solution of the architrave detail is completely original, creating a perfect balance between the forces and resistance of the components of which it is made up. This ring rests on a torus (the curved vault of the gallery) which carries perfectly the outward thrust of the stones like a continuous flying buttres, one part resting on the outer walls and the other on the ring-beam. When this wall is weakened by an opening, as occurs on the west side, the extra load is carried by a lower vault or some other means of buttressing.

The upper level of the court, with Ionic columns of the same stone as those on the ground floor, was roofed in 1967 with a wooden "Artesonado". The deep box-moulding and radical beams could easily have been the work of Pedro Machuca himself. The same occurs with the staircase in the south-east corner leading to the Museo de Bellas Artes. With its bold curves this far surpasses the original seventeenth century one in the opposite corner, despite its modernity.

Attempts have been made to find precedents for the plan of this building. It has been written that it was inspired by the Palace of Caprarola by Vignola, but it must be remembered that that palace with its pentagonal plan and circular court, was built in 1546 while Machuca's project is almost twenty years earlier.

A special mention must be made of the so-called "Crypt" which was mentioned in relation to the Patio de los Arrayanes. This is to be found under the unfinished chapel in the north-east corner of the renaissance court. It is now reached by a stairway in the vestibule on the east side. It has an octagonal vault, almost flat in section and star-shaped in plan, and has no other form of support other than its own curvature. This can without any doubt be considered one of the works of genius of the Renaissance.

THE GENERALIFE

O f the pleasure gardens on the Cerro del Sol the Generalife is the only one to survive to the present day. It was an estate where the King of Granada retired, away from the preocupations of the Court. Its proximity to the Alhambra (apart from the advantage of one being close to the centre of government and thus being able to attend to urgent matters during the holidays) was also a sign of the richness of the owner: when transport was by mule or on foot a recreational estate so near to one's permanent residence was an indication that the owner was very rich. The opulence of the owner was in direct relation to the proximity of his country house.

The meaning of the name "Generalife" is obscured in utter confusion. Yannat al-'arif, so says Ibn Aljatib, means "principal 'huerta' " (small holding or country garden), according to Seco de Lucena. "Huerta of the Architect" say other authors without realising that "alarife" is a term which takes in many activities, apart from the one they mention. Are any of the Architects of the Alhambra known? Since the designers of the palaces have been conspicuously ignored in the inscription in the palaces, it seems strange to dedicate the most important gardens in Granada, if not the whole kingdom,to one of them.

Because of the shortness of this work we will have to leave aside the many versions of the origin of the name Generalife, but we cannot resist giving at least one of our 'crop': the function of the Generalife is that of a "carmen" (Granada house in the city, with a garden) the residence where the people of Granada went in the autumn, the most beautiful season in this region. At that time the temperature is mild with neither oppressive heat of summer nor the dry cold of winter. There are still flowers in the gardens, blue skies and little rain most days. If we accept that the root *"Yannat"* is prominent in the majority of the theories, why not *Yannat al-jarif* or "the autumn garden"?

The Generalife was given by the Reyes Católicos to the 'comendador' (Warden) Hinestrosa. By a series of inheritances and marriages, etc. it came into the hands of the Granada Venegas family, thence finally to the Marqueses of Campotejar who were related to the Grimaldi-Palavicini from Milan. Following a long court case in which the State claimed ownership of the Generalife, the case was found in favour of the owners, who ceded the palace to the Spanish State without cost, in 1921. For this act of generosity Alfonso XIII created the title of Marques del Generalife.

All that remains of the original gardens are the terraces where they were planted. These workings reached to the top of the mount so that, from the top, one saw them as one entity down to the foot of the hill, with the variety of colours which the flowers and fruit trees imprinted on each of the steps. The present gardens have nothing in common with Medieval Gardens where flowers and fruits were mixed heterogeneously. In the present gardens only the senses of smell and sight are played upon. In the Mussulman garden one enjoyed the sight of the flowers, their perfume, the sound of water and the taste of the fruit eaten as one passed under the trees. This was a "huerta", a word difficult to translate into many languages, from the Latin 'hortus' and which was the common description of what today we call "jardín" or garden.

In the fourteenth century, Ibn Luyun enumerated the conditions that an estate of this kind should fulfil:

"For the location of an house amidst gardens choose ye a hillock which makes easy its care and protection. The building shall face the noonday, and be at the entrance to the estate, and at the highest place make a well or pond, or better yet make a canal which runs in the shade. The house should have but two doors, so that it is most protected and thus the inhabitants shall have greater rest".

All these conditions are found in what remains of the much-altered residence around the so called Patio de la Acequia (Court of the Canal or reservoir). The 'canal', which runs North-South along the spine of the court has, since the romantic period, two rows of spouts which, form water arches cascading into the canal in the Italianate manner. In this way the mirror effect which the pond had in the time of the Nazaries is broken and the air is filled with obsessive noise made as the fountains hit the surface of the water. In the original design the water entered from the two fountains at the ends of the pool, forming a pleasant murmur, like calming music which does not interfere with one's thoughts.

In the time of the Reyes Catolicos some arches were opened in the western wall of the court, and its height was lowered. In the Islamic period there was only one opening in the wall, the pavillion at the middle.

The North end, the best preserved, is fronted by an arcade

of round-headed arches. The centre one greater in height. These three arches of similar design are the entrance to a transverse space, covered with a wooden 'lazo' ceiling. This is the antichambre to a gazebo placed slightly off-centre, to the right of the line of the central canal. There are five small windows above the three arches. The presence of a poem

around them painted on a lapis lazuli blue ground and making mention of king Abu-l-Walid Ismail and of "the year of the triumph of religion"... dates this building to the year 1319.

Translated by David H. Beaman

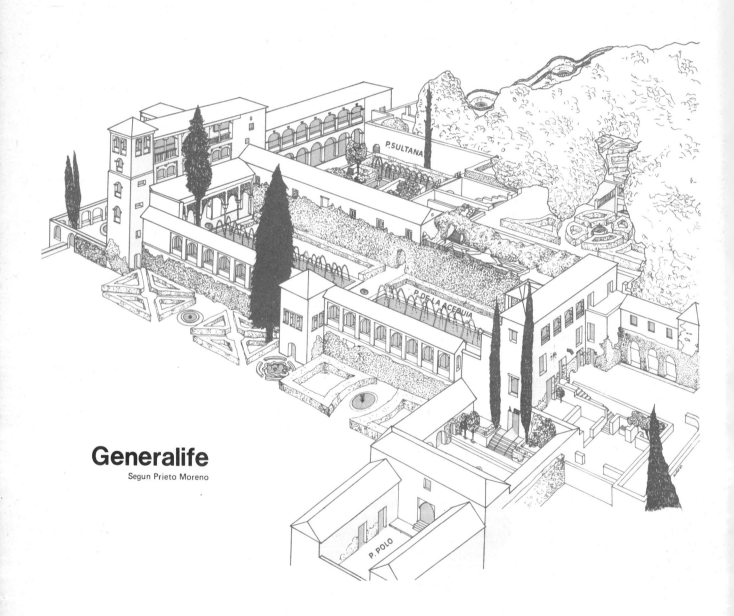

Generalife
Segun Prieto Moreno

Edición y realización: *Juan Agustín Núñez para Capitel, S.C.A.* Fotografía: *Miguel Román Vega y J. Agustín Núñez.* Material empleado: *Kodachrome 100 Plus-Profesional.* Revelado: *E-6 Goyo Fotocolor (Granada).* Dibujos: *José M.ª Medina y Xavier Bosch.* Montaje: *David Medina.* Fotocomposición: *Computext y Walter de Fanti.* Fotomecánica: *Infosag, S.A.* Impresión: *Mateu Cromo.*

ISSBN: 84-87282-51-2   Inglés   Dep. Legal: G R. 1.925-89

Sala de Dos Hermanas — Hall of the two Sisters — Salle de Deux Soeurs — Raum der Zwei Schwestern — Salla delle due Sorelle.

Patio de los Leones: Detalle — Detail — Détail — Detail — Particolare

Cúpula de la Sala de dos Hermanas — Dome of the two Sister's room — Plafond de la salle de "Deux Soeurs" — Kuppel des Saals der Zwei Schwestern — Sofitto della salla delle due Sorelle

Partal

Baños
Baths
Les Bains
Die Bäder
Bagno

←

Torre de las Infantas

Generalife

Pags. 60-64: **Palacio de Carlos V, detalles** — Palace of Charles the V, details — Palace de Charles V, détailles — Palast von Karl V, Details — Palazzo di Carolo V, particolari

GRANADA CRISTIANA

Granada, "a delight to the eye and a comfort to the soul" —was so described by an Arab poet, before it passed into the hands of the Christians. Long before being reconquered in 1492, it was coveted for its unequaled natural beauty, for the magnificence of its palaces, and for its impressive fortress of the Alhambra.

Much before 1492 and the fall of the city and its occupation by the Christians, they were bent upon possessing rather than destroying Granada. In order to understand the history of this city, (both Moslem and Christian), we must keep in mind the eight centuries of strife between them. This yearning for possesion is born of a desire to make of this city a historic symbol, and because of this, is created a compendium of great Renaissance and Baroque works of art, that continue the fame and beauty attained during the Moslem Middle Ages.

To understand the reality of this city we must realize that Christian Granada is a symbiosis of Moorish and Christian (Morisco and Mudejar) cultures. In most cases the greatest achievements of the new image of the city, created in the Renaissance and Baroque periods and later in the Romantic period of the XIX century, arise from the rich inheritance of the Nazarite period. It is a pity that the twentieth century city has not known, for the most part, how to make urban renewal compatible with modernization and respect for the past. The towers of the Alhambra, high above the city, tell us part of the tale. The rest is told by the towers and cupola of the Cathedral, the Renaissance and Baroque churches and the convents of the Albaycin. All this is surrounded by the luxuriant beauty of the vega (the valley) and the massive and impressive Sierra Nevada with its frosty peaks of Mulhacen and Veleta.

How shall we approach Christian Granada? Shall we follow the steps of the protagonists: the conquerers, the so called +Catholic Monarchs—, Carlos V, or their heirs and governors? Better yet: let's visit the monuments which have beautified and universalized Granada.

Coat-of-arms of Spain
The exterior cresting
of the
Royal Chapel.

67

Retablo. Royal Chapel Main Altar. Work of the sculptor Philippe de Vigarny, (1520-1522), with scenes of the Passion of Christ on the upper level and on the middle level scenes of Saints John the Baptist and Evangelist. The Adoration of the Magi on the central lower level. Under this reliefs of the surrender of Granada and the baptism of the Moors. On the sides the praying figures of the Catholic Monarchs. All in polychromed wood.

Detail of the tomb of the Catholic Monarchs.

THE RENAISSANCE AND THE BAROQUE PERIOD

Triumphant with the conquest of Granada, Fernando and Isabel soon organize endowments for the creation of monuments that will make apparent to all, the true historical importance of their feat, not only for the city of Granada but for all the nation. While planning the construction of a Cathedral over the Major Mosque of the city they first establish a provisional one in the Mosque of the Alhambra on May 21, 1492.

By 1501 the Catholic Monarchs had decreed that all the properties and patrimony of all the mosques of Granada should be endowed to the yet to be built Cathedral.

But by far the greatest legacy left to the city by the Catholic Monarchs was the decision to build in the city the chapel to be known as «de los Reyes» (of the Monarchs), that was to be their final resting place. Desirous of making this city the symbol of their greatest political dreams, they decreed in Medina del Campo on September 13, 1504 that in the new Cathedral a chapel should be built «at the right hand of the Main Chapel and patronized by the SS John the Baptist and John the Evangelist. It was established that in perpetuity this chapel would be attended by thirteen chaplains who would offer three daily masses for their

souls and those of their ancestors and heirs. That three anniversary masses would be celebrated after their demise and on all All Saints Day. They also decreed that in this chapel should be placed the Blessed Sacrament, and before it, day and night, perpetually, a six pound candle should be lit and two oil lamps should be placed specifically for the devotion to the Sacrament.

After founding the Chapel, they ordered in their testaments, that should they die before the completion of the Chapel, they should be taken to the monastery of San Francisco in the Alhambra to be interred until the Royal Chapel should be ready to receive them. Isabel died in 1504 and Fernando in 1516 but it was not until the 10th of November of 1521 that the conquerers of Granada were taken to their final resting place, in a solemn procession from the Alhambra to the newly consacrated Chapel.

The key to an era, the design and building of the Royal Chapel, were commissioned to Enrique Egas, the major architect of the Catholic Monarchs, on the 30th of October 1506. His design of great simplicity and austerity was probably made following the desires of Cardenal Cisneros and the Queen herself. But this simplicity was later to displease the representati-

CAPILLA REAL

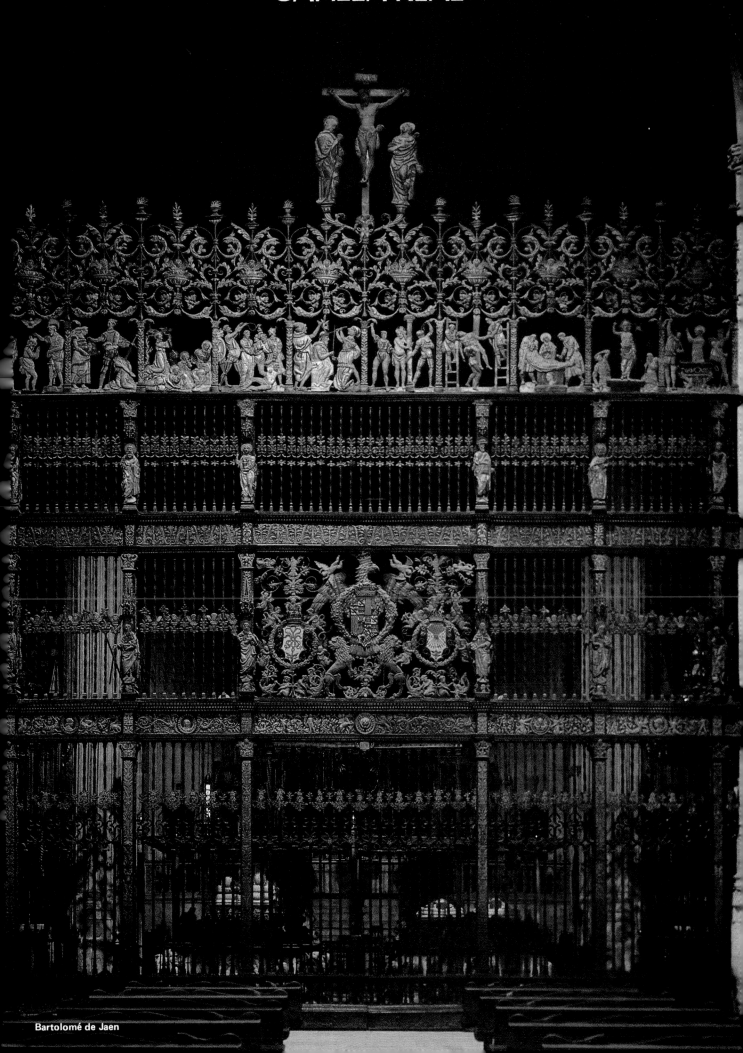

Bartolomé de Jaen

Bartolomé Ordoñez

Mausoleos. D.ª Juana y D. Felipe

Mausoleos. D. Fernando y Doña Isabel

Domenico Fancelli

Below: Details of the showcases of the sacristy of the Royal Chapel with pendants and flags of the Christian armies. Jewelery and sacred ornaments embroidered in gold.

Preceding page left: Tomb of Philip the Fair and Juana la Loca. Sculptured by Bartolomé Ordóñez in Carrara marble (1519-1520). Side and angled views. Royal Chapel.

Tomb of the Catholic Monarchs, Fernando and Isabel. Work of the Italian sculptor Domenico Alessandro Fancelli (1517) realized in Carrara marble. Side and angled views. Royal Chapel.

tive of the Monarch and Carlos V, himself, who considered that the glory of his grandparents merited a more grandiose treatment.

The Chapel, of Latin Cross design, with elevated choir, is a fine example of Isabelline Gothic; less luxurious than the Chapel of San Juan de los Reyes in Toledo, and smaller than the Chapel of Santo Tomas in Avila.

The style of the Chapel and its proportions, the cresting on its outer walls, Isabel's and Fernando's shields and initials, which are found on the southern and only exterior façade of the building, are clear examples of late Gothic with early indications of Renaissance style. All this is a clear manifestation of the modernity of the Catholic Monarchs and their heirs.

Its original main entrance, on the north side, and inside the Cathedral is an excellent example of Ogival art with many royal crests, initials with crowned yoke and arrows and a dedication that reads «Laudet eam opera eius» (May their works be praised). It is formed by a semi-circular ornamented arch at whose sides stand the images of the SS John the Baptist and Evangelist and heralds carrying staffs which seems to convert the opening in a triumphal arch. It is believed that Enrique Egas directed the work and that the sculptures were done by the great pre-renaissance artist, Jorge Fernández.

The entrance at the foot of the Chapel is of interest as it connects with the ancient Nasrite Mesquita, used

as a cathedral before the construction of the modern one. Today it connects with the baroque church of El Sagrario. Of special value, flanking the doorway are the lovely stone polychromed figures of St. Peter and St. Paul who symbolically seem to be guarding the church.

The third entrance opened in the exterior wall in 1527, some years after the completion of the chapel, is of Plateresque style and was probably designed by Juan García de Praves. Only the upper part remains as originally designed. The Portal and the adjacent Lonja contrast with the Gothic design and decoration of the rest of the façade; the repetition of the Royal initials in the ornamental stone filigree balustrades, the gargoyles and the miniature pinnacles with their crockets. The lower half of the doorway is a poor XVII century restoration, but the imperial seal with its two-headed eagle in the center continues to symbolize the royal foundation of this building. Each detail seems to call out the courtly character of this place —the essence of the new city—aulic Christian constructions in the heart of Moslem Granada, surrounded by the Mesquita, Madraza, Fonde and commercial center.

The interior of the monument, in accord with its funerary character, is a private and public place. Its private and solemn character is accentuated by its proportions, subdued lighting, the chromatic tones of the whole and originally by the gilded Gothic letters on its walls and its polychromed royal crests which unfortu-

Above: Detail of the left side of the triptych of the «retablo de Santa Cruz» with the Crucifixion of Christ. Transept of the Royal Chapel. Work of the paintor Dierick Bouts (1420-1475).

nately were white washed in 1838 and then cleaned and left in the bare stone at the end of the XIX century.

Round the walls runs an inscription in gilded Gothic characters stating that the Catholic Monarchs had conquered Granada and converted it to their faith, that they had built churches, monasteries and hospitals and that they had expelled the Moors.

In the geometric center of the transept are the Royal tombs with their effigies in Carrara marble made by the Italian sculptor Domenico Alexandro Fancelli. This harmonious but monumental work was commissioned by the Emperor Carlos V in honour of his grandparents. It contrasts greatly with the simple tomb that Isabel had invisioned, as can be seen below in the crypt.

LA REJA (Iron Grill)

The magnificent Reja, the work of Master Bartolomé in 1520, is one of the finest grill works in all of Spain, and a most singular chapter in Spanish Renaissance art. The light at dusk, in the silent temple seems to set the polychromed and gilded part of the grill aflame, stretching its transparent web across the nave before the transept and is for this reason farther forward than the usual chancel screen. The filtered light rests upon the solemn tombs and on the sculptured elements of the great retablo of Felipe de Vigarni. Except for the open central panel the reja separates the royal sepulchral monument from the nave. In it all the fantasies of Plateresque art are expressed.

Divided in three storeys, the lowest has six Corinthian columns with Plateresque adornments supporting the royal arms, angels, intertwined foliage, and on the columns are figures of the apostles on pedestals and crowned with Gothic canopies, motif which also decorates the third level. Above this, rises the masterpiece of sculpture in iron, ten episodes from the life of Christ, the martydoms of SS John the Baptist and Evangelist and towering above all, in the center, the Crucifixion. Part of the reja's magnificence is most certainly due to the proximity of vertical and horizontal straight lines and to the intricate ornamental patterns in iron.

THE TOMB AND THE RETABLO

Above the crypt are the two impressive catafalques in marble. The sepulchral monuments of the Catholic Monarchs, to the right, are the work of the Italian Fancelli. They were carved in Genoa, finished in 1517 in Granada and placed in 1522. Of Carrara marble of exceptional quality and tone the tomb of the Catholic Monarchs is according to Bertaux «the union of Florentine grace and Spanish grandeur». Atop the monument are the recumbent figures with serene profiles slightly turned away from another; Isabel is wearing a tunic and cloak and hanging from a chain a medallion of the Order of Santiago. Fernando is wearing a full suit of armour, partially covered with a cloak and about his neck a medaillon with a relief of Saint George. The monument has a quadrangular base with inclined sides decorated with figures of the apostles and at the four corners are fantastical griffins with lions claws and eagle wings.

Among the Greeks the griffins were thought to be guardian monsters who protected treasures while the Christians considered them to be cruel and evil forces. Above each griffin is a saint —four guardians of the Church— St. Agustine, St. Jerome, St. Ambroise and St. Gregory— who probably represented the triumph of Christianity over paganism. The theme is treated repeatedly throughout the sculpture with allegories of Pegasus, Centurions, Phoenix, skulls, and these symbols combined with political ones such as the pomegranate, lion, castle, and yoke and arrow.

On each side of the lower level we have representations of the Resurrection, the Baptism of Christ, Saint George and Saint James. On three sides of the upper level are royal seals carried by angels and on the fourth side, at their feet, is an inscription that boasts that Fernando and Isabel had expelled the Moors from Granada. At the foot of each figure and as though guarding their eternal sleep are a lion and a lioness. In conclusion, it was with this sepulchre that

Central detail of the triptych of the «retablo of Santa Cruz». Outstanding work of the Flamish paintor Dierick Bouts (1420-1475). The descention of the Cross, one of the most important works of the Royal Chapel.

a long period of change ends and a modern era begins. The renaissance tomb under the dome of a Gothic chapel are the happy evidence of the political-cultural moment.

On the left is the tomb of Juana la Loca and her husband Felipe the Fair. The work was commissioned to Bartolmé Ordóñez by Carlos V in 1519. The sculptor, clearly influenced by Michelangelo, is considered one of the four greatest artists of the Spanish Renais-

sance. Most of his work was done in Italy and for Italy. While working on this sepulchre, at Carrara, he died before it was completed.

The work of this colleague of Diego de Siloé is similar in style to Fancelli's as is confirmed by the great sculptural monument. In contrast to the serenity of the figures of the Catholic Monarchs, Ordóñez bestows upon his work qualities of greater plastic movement and more daring contrasts. This funerary monu-

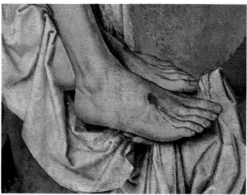

Detail of the right sight of the tryptich of the «retablo de Santa Cruz». Transept of the Royal Chapel. It represents the Resurrection of Christ.

ment has high vertical walls upon which rests a tomb on which lie the recumbant figures. The Monarchs richly attired, he with a sword and she with a scepter, have idealized profiles. The Queen's countenance has especially inspired poets over the centuries as in the case of Federico García Lorca who praises her beauty in «Elegy to Juana la Loca».

On the lower part of the base are circular reliefs depicting scenes related to the life of Christ and twelve niches separated by balustered columns in which are placed the seven virtues and five allegories. Of special note are Fortitude, Temperance, Theology and Mathematics. On the high corners, beside the King he has finished a sculpture of St. Andrew and left St. Michael roughly prepared. Beside the Queen are the two Johns. On the lower part are mythical figures and the symbols of the Monarchs, a chain for the Duchy of Burgandy and the yoke and arrows and granada (Pomegrenate) for the heirs of the Catholic Monarchs. On the side of the feet is a lovely XVIII century epitaph supported by angels that expounds the virtues of this King and Queen and explains that they are the parents of the Emperor Carlos V who ordered the construction of this monument.

Because this tomb is higher than the other it gives an unbalanced front view. This can lead us to believe as suggest XVI century documents that this second tomb was meant to be placed elsewhere in the chapel or even in the Cathedral itself. Only a lateral view from the right side of the transept allows us to view both works jointly.

Beneath these sepulchers is the burial crypt under an austere vault of stone. The lead caskets are placed with awesome simplicity on plain slabs of quarry stone. Seeing this simplicity one understands the original intention and request made by Queen Isabel in the second clause of her testament. She states therein that she wishes to be buried with the greatest simplicity and without pomp and that all that would have been spent on such ceremonies be given to the poor.

In the crypt today are, in the center, the caskets with the remains of Queen Isabel and of King Fernando. At the sides are those of Queen Juana la Loca and King Felipe the Fair and a small coffin which contains the remains of Prince Miguel, a grandchild of the Catholic Monarchs and son of Isabel, the oldest daughter of the Monarchs, and the King of Portugal.

Because of the unexpected death of this child the crown of Aragon and Castilla passed into the hands of prince Carlos, son of Juana and Felipe. Other mem-

76

The Nativity of Christ, painted by the flemish master Van der Weyden, (1399-1464). It was part of the tryptich previously mentioned. Of special importance because of its great technical quality, chromatic richness and majestic use of light and space. Museum of the Sacristy. Royal Chapel.

bers of the Royal family were buried here until 1574 when they were all transferred to El Escorial, which replaced Granada as the site of the Royal Pantheon.

Facing the tombs is a wide marble stairway flanked by ornate marble handrails carved with foliage and grotesque figures, the creation of the Italian Francisco Florentin.

Dominating all of the chapel and especially the presbytery, over the main altar and at the head of the stairs, is the great retablo of Felipe de Vigarni. The work is one of the first in Plateresque style in Spain. Its architectural and decorative format is noteworthy but most outstanding is the sculptural work.

The gilding of the patrons, Saint John the Baptist and the Evangelist, is excellent and also noteworthy is the Adoration of the Magi, in the center and at bench height, is the resemblance of the youngest king to Carlos V.

At the sides of the retablo are the Catholic Monarchs *orantes*, (praying) an idealized though excellent work of Diego de Siloé. Fernando is placed next to the panel of the surrender of Granada with King Boabdil handing over the keys of the city to the Cath-

olic Monarchs and Isabel next to the relief, on the right, which shows the conversion of the Moors.

The retablo is the backcloth that closes all of this iconographic program of glorification and commemoration of the people and events that protagonized the first glorious days of modern Christian Granada. Only the work of the great Spanish Renaissance sculptor and artist Alonso de Berruguete is missing. There are critics who, however, find evidence of his style in the expressive and overwhelming scenes of the Martydom of Saint John and Christ carrying the Cross on the left side of the retablo, which are totally different from all the work on the right side.

OTHER RETABLOS
AND THE SACRISTY MUSEUM

At the transept and during the baroque period were added two magnificent retablos in which are incorporated cupboards and reliquaries. The many carvings and paintings are the work of Alonso de Mena and

were completed in 1632. In the interior are an important number of paintings on wood and relics, as well as jewels which belonged to the Catholic Monarchs who donated them for this Chapel. On these retablos and on its benches, are the carved portraits of the Monarchs, D. Felipe, Doña Juana, Carlos V, the empress Isabel, Felipe IV and his wife Isabel de Borbon. The richness of the gilded and polychromed Baroque work of these retablos, contrasts greatly with the marble tombs and the other retablo of the Holy Cross, which is at the left of the transept and is the work of Jacobo Florentino in 1521. It was made for the magnificent *Triptych of the Passion* by Dierick Bouts. This belonged to Queen Isabel and it is, without a doubt, the most treasured and beautiful work of all of the Chapel. The Descent from the Cross, perfection of colour and sensibility in its entirely, is flanked on the right by the Crucifixion and on the left by the Resurrection. This work and the benches, by Pedro Machuca and Florentin, were all carefully restored and placed here in 1945.

On the other side of the transept is the Isabelline entrance of the sacristy, today the Treasury of the Chapel. Herein is a museum of art works and momentos of great artistic and historic value. Historically of great significance are the crown and scepter of the Queen and the florentine sword with which King Fer-

nuary, through the streets of Granada to commemorate the surrender of the city by the Moors.
were to be carried each year, on the second day of January, through the streets of Granada to commemorate the surrender of the city by the Moors.

In addition to these important treasures are banners, pennants, standards and flags that belonged to the Castillian armies during the War of Granada. We can see as well chalices and vestments embroidered in gold, that were also donated by the Catholic Monarchs for their Chapel. The Queen's mirror, converted into a monstrance, and then returned to its original state is here too.

There are numerous works of the Flemish school and others by Spanish and Italian masters. Of the exhibited works —outstanding among the best— is a set of two panels, the Pieta and the Nativity, of a triptych by the great Flemish master Van der Weyden. The third section, the Resurrection, is in the New York Metropolitan Museum. In this great work of Marian theme the artist offers the three most crucial moments in the life of the Virgin with relation to Jesus Christ: Birth, Death and Resurrection. After his experience as a sculptor, Van der Weyden, inspired by his masters the Van Eycks, knew how to transmit in his paintings all of the unrestrained power of the new approach to interpreting art. In this work, especially in

Hans Memling

Enthroned Virgen nursing the Christchild by Hans Memling. The richness of colours and the tenderness of the scene give special interest to this work. Museum of the sacristy. Royal Chapel.

80

Above: Holy women. A triptych of the Descent by the Flemish master Hans Memling (1435-1494). Tenderness characterizes this master even in themes of sorrow. Museum of the sacristy. Royal Chapel.

the Pietá, he offers us his most categorically vigorous and creative style. His forceful palette dramatically emphasizes the clear diagonal between the body of Christ upon the black cloak of the Virgin accentuating the tragic union of the two heads. The background of this painting, differs from the triptych of the same theme that is in the Prado Museum in Madrid.

The contemplation of these outstanding works requires time and concentration. The pleasure of the aesthetic works combined with the historic significance of this chapel has attracted travellers from all over the world. Visitors, who come to appreciate this Granada of the Catholic Monarchs, this fusion and contrast of two cultures: the Alhambra with its Royal Palaces and this sepulchral chapel, treasury and museum. Here in the intimacy of this chapel our imaginations take flight and we clearly perceive the splendour of renaissance Granada with relation to Europe and America. Certainly, we should recall here that these Monarchs, Fernando and Isabel, together with Christopher Colombus, began in this city one of man's most important exploits: the discovery of America.

Detail of Christ's portrait by Dierick Bouts, (1420-1475). Museum of the Sacristy. Royal Chapel.

View of the Cathedral from the northside. The architectural value of the unfinished tower and the great Absis rise above the neighboring buildings and stand out against Sierra Nevada in the background.

THE
CATHEDRAL

This part of the city, called by the Moslems «of Hara Alchama» (of the Major Mosque) was chosen by the Catholic Monarchs to build the first and most important Christian temples. First, the Mezquita (today the Sagrario) was consecrated and dedicated to Our Lady of O. Later, on its north side was planned the construction of the actual Cathedral and next to it, as we have already seen, the Royal Chapel. Thus, this place which has been the heart of Moslem life, became the nub of the new Christian city.

The nearby *Madraza* (Moslem religious school) was founded in about 1349 by King Yusuf I and was, without a doubt, one of the most important buildings of the Nasarite city. After the Christian conquest the Catholic Monarchs granted the building to the city, and from 1500 to 1851 it was the Town Hall. Today this building has a lovely XVIII century facade and a superb mudejar hall. In the mid XIX century, when this building became too small for the needs of the Town Hall, the *Ayuntamiento* was moved to the Convent of the Carmelitas Calzadas in the present day Plaza del Carmen. This convent was built in 1627 over the her-

mitage of Nuestra Señora de la Cabeza which had existed there prior to 1572.

The Plaza de Bibrambla, (expanded between 1516 and 1519), the walls of the city and the Alcaiceria (silk bazaar), bordered this district on the west. Parallel to the right bank of the River Darro, was the Zacatin, the most important street in the city. Modern XX century urban renewal on the north side and the opening of the Gran Via, slowly transformed this medieval quarter of narrow and intercrossed streets. In Nasarite times it was, without a doubt, one of the most important and populated parts of the city.

In this district, close to the Mezquita, as we have said, was planned the construction of the new Cathedral. A Gothic design was most definitely planned, inspired by the Cathedral of Toledo, when Enrique Egas was commissioned in 1518 to take charge of the floor plan. This district was clearly intended to be Gothic as can be seen in the Royal Chapel and in the old Lonja (Exchange), which were undertaken in the same year, intermixing Gothic, Mudejar and Plateresque styles. However, once the foundations were laid for the Cathedral a Renaissance style was chosen, making it the first in Spain in the new style.

From the 25th of March 1523, when the first stone was placed, until 1528 Enrique Egas and Sebastian de Alcantara directed the construction of the Gothic Cathedral. At this time Egas was relieved of his post. It appears that the new artistic trends apparent in the city, where much new construction was underway, was soon to affect the style of the new Cathedral. At that time Jacobo Florentino was working on the church-monastery of San Jeronimo and Pedro Machuca on the palace of Carlos V in the Alhambra. These buildings along with the decoration of the Royal Chapel, in the new Renaissance style, were receiving much enthusiastic interest.

Diego de Siloé, from Burgos, had come to Granada to work on the church of San Jeronimo, as well as on the tomb of D. Gonzalo Fernández de Cordova, El Gran Capitan of the Reyes Catolicos. He was put in charge of the new Renaissance project for the Cathedral.

The decision of the town council to change the style of the new Cathedral caused quite a stir and many misgivings within certain circles. Most important, however, was the King's disapproval, as stated in a Royal Order sent to the Cabildo at the end of 1528. Among other reasons the Monarch felt that the change in style would be detrimental to the Royal Chapel.

On the 9th of January 1529 Diego de Siloé, sponsored by the archbishop of Toledo, D. Alonso de Fonseca, defended his project before the Monarch. His presentation was apparently successful, the new project was approved, and work continued on the new Cathedral.

Siloé utilized the piers and pedestals of the pilasters in the exterior walls, the distribution of the transept and probably, the width and length of the original project. The changes made by Siloé in the rest of the foundation and the remaining structure are a clear example of a Renaissance church rising from a Gothic floor plan. The interior of the temple consists of five aisles supported by twenty enormous pillars, flanked by Corinthian columns that raise its dome to a height of 30 meters.

The *Capilla Mayor* is one of the most superb constructions of this kind in Spain. The circular structure housing the high altar is the masterpiece of Siloé's work. It is extremely high, (45 meters) overwhelmingly graceful, and transmits a luminous clarity. The cupola is sustained by twelve thick Corinthian pillars, which valiently adapt their arches to the curvature of the dome.

It is connected to the ambulatory by seven openings between the piers, now closed by the choir which was placed around the altar in 1926. At that time it was moved from its usual position in the central aisle.

Siloé's solutions to technical problems, thanks to his genius, become aesthetic successes. The monumental nature of the main chapel, of colossal dimensions and intent, is in harmony and proportion thanks to the use of a series of modulating units; plinths, co-

lumns attached to pilasters and round arches, perfectly spaced up to the dome, with prominent ribs that accentuate the exactness of the space.

As is to be expected, especially inside, all of this area is covered with religious imagery. Affixed to the 12 columns of the chapel, in Baroque style, are the figures of the apostles, like the pillars upon which Christ built his Church. From the bottom to the top, including the stained glass windows, we have an iconographic interpretation of the Redemption of Christ. On the columns of the second level are seven large paintings by Alonso Cano of episodes in the life of the Virgin. The stained glass windows from Flanders are painted in part by Theodore of Holland and include the Transfiguration, the Last Supper and the Crucifixion.

The treatment of the entire chapel is a triumphal one, both in its architectural aspects as well as in its decoration.

The rest of Siloé's project is clearly Renaissance, both in its floor plan as well as in its elevation. The choir was placed in the center of the main aisle, as was the main transept; in front of the main chapel, at a tangent to the great circle of the dome, and crossing the temple at its widest point. The other transept is in the ambulatory, covering only three aisles. Siloé's project ends with a façade that has a triple triumphal arch and two towers.

Its clear conception is confirmed in its classic proportions and in the richness of its iconographic symbolism. Justifiably this monument is a model and example for other great Andalusian Renaissance cathedrals.

The exterior beauty of the whole monument, especially the Main Chapel and ambulatory, was once a special part of the Granada landscape. Before it became surrounded by buildings that have destroyed its majesty, it once inspired poets and painters. A lovely drawing of its profile, by Velazquez gives us a clear picture of its grandiosity.

THE PORTALS

Diego de Siloé, architect and sculptor, completed the monument with portals as rich in sculptural elements as in solutions to architectural composition. Such is the case with the *Ecce Homo*, in the Main Chapel, the entrance to the Sacristy and above all, the Puerta del Perdon, on the north side. This plateresque portal, done between 1535 and 1538 was completed almost a century before the main, or west portal designed by Alonso Cano, in Baroque style.

In the Puerta del Perdon with its noble proportions and fine artistic work we find one of Siloé's loveliest creations. Above the central arch we have the figures of Faith and Justice, considered by some, the best of Siloé's work.

The tablet between the two figures bears the following inscription: «After 700 years of Moslem domination, we both (Faith and Justice) gave these dominions to the Catholic Sovereigns: within this temple are their bodies and their souls have gone to heaven,

84

CATEDRAL

D. Siloe

Stained-glass windows of the Cathedral: In the upper section of the Main Chapel some very beautyful stain-glass windows represent the life of Christ. Work of Juan von Kamp, XVI century (right).

THE INTERIOR DECORATION

because they acted with justice and faith».

On the lateral pillars are shields held by angels; on the right, the imperial crest of Carlos V and on the left the crest of the Catholic Monarchs.

Until his death in 1563 Siloé remained in charge of the work, completing the Capilla Mayor and ambulatory and beginning the naves from the transept. The first mass was celebrated in 1561.

In 1666, almost a century later, in the Baroque period, the main entrance was created by Alonso Cano. Cano's design, continued after his death by José Granados de la Barrera, and later by Melchor de Aguirre at the end of the 18th century, is roughly a Roman triumphal arch with its impressive central entrance flanked by smaller arches on each side. Its well proportioned masses stand out boldly, giving the chiaroscuro effect that Cano so often achieved in his paintings. Cano conceived the portal as a great retablo in which the sculptural elements and decorative ones play a double roll: the iconographic and the dynamic-aesthetic one. The assorted sculpture is mostly by Verdiguier and his son.

All of this work belongs to a moment in the history of the church when the monumental nature of the exterior was used to attract the attention and emotion of the faithful, thus creating a holy space in the plaza that stands before the temple.

All the unrestrained feeling of the façade is found in the interior of the Cathedral in its rich collection of Baroque retablos of the XVIII century, among which stand out the unique piece by Duque Cornejo of Nuestra Señora de la Antigua; one of Santiago; the one of the altar of Jesus of Nazareth, all profusely gilded and with original design in sculpture as well as painting. Also of note, are the large Baroque organs and pulpits, worked in marble and engraved in gold by the architect Francisco Hurtado Izquierdo, and the magnificent marble and polychromed retablo of Nuestra Señora de las Angustias.

Neoclassicism is represented by three retablos of importance: la Virgen del Pilar, by Francisco Aguado in 1785; those in the Chapel of San Cecilio, dedicated to the patron Saint of the city, and those to the co-patrons San Juan de Dios, on the right, and to San Emigidio (defender against earthquakes) on the left, also designed by Francisco Aguado and sculpted by Verdiguier. The static equilibrium of the neoclassic works appear as a chapter in parenthesis next to the Baroque and the elegance of the whole Cathedral.

The work of Alonso Cano, as painter and sculptor, stands out in this monument. Among all his works, and possibly the most appealing in this cathedral, is a miniature carved Inmaculada. Today in the Sacristy, it was originally made for the lectern in the choir, and is one of the key pieces of the Spanish Baroque period.

Interior of the central nave of the Cathedral. Main Chapel.

It is not possible here to pretend to point out all of the painted works and canvases in this cathedral. We can only suggest the importance of this monument as a center of Renaissance and Baroque art.

OTHER MONUMENTS

Renaissance Granada is also represented by many other civil and religious monuments. The Palace of Castril (today the Provincial Archeological Museum), the Royal Hospital or the lovely portal of the Lonja, to name a few, are all illustrative of the Plateresque style.

While the impressive Palaces of Calahorra and Carlos V of the Alhambra (studied in a previous volume) are defined as examples of renaissance architecture in its purest forms.

The completion of the Royal Chapel in 1521, attracted many of the best national and international artists who were enthusiastic about the new Romanesque style. Masters such as Alonso de Berruguete, Jacobo Florentino and Pedro Machuca, painter, author and architect of the Palace of Carlos V of the Alhambra, had come to Granada, interested in the works in progress in the new imperial city. The Emperor, Carlos

V, in 1526 came with his bride, Isabel de Portugal. They arrived with an entourage that included ambassadors, diplomats, secretaries, ladies-in-waiting, artists, poets... All had come to the new Christian city to see first hand the marvels that were being created here. Diego de Siloé was here also, in charge of the building of the church of San Jernónimo. In 1521 a Royal decree had granted the Gran Capitan's wife, the use of this new temple as the final resting place for this great national hero and leader.

In essence, but on a larger scale, the floor plan repeats the form of the Royal Chapel's sanctuary. Both in the location of the transept as well as in the form of the nave and its chapels. Originally conceived in Gothhic style it was continued by Jacobo Florentino in Renaissance style, employing in the interior ribbed Corinthian pilasters and outside grouping the buttresses in pyramidal form with modular structures and cornices.

In 1528 Siloé is called to take charge of the works. Commissioned to close the sanctuary, he is given total freedom in the planning of all architectural, sculptural and artistic work in the temple.

He began with the second floor plan of the temple although his greatest innovation was the completion of the transept. The cupola is mounted on four ribbed arches on which are the figures of the four Evangelists from which spring four flared arches. While the style is not at all classic, it is harmonious and balanced. These stylistic solutions inside, combined with the exterior work (spaced buttresses, triple arched windows, coat-of-arms and figures), all create a monument, which shares its religious function with its vigorous desire to glorify the memory of El Gran Capitan. The figurative themes of the sculptures and the tablets with their inscriptions, all accentuate this intention.

En 1547 Siloé contracted the choir stalls and still with some Gothic elements, created a lovely pair of portals for the large cloister completed in 1519. He also completed the fine ornamentation at the base of the main façade and of the tower. This tower was dismantled by the French at the beginning of the XIX century in order to construct a bridge. In 1963 the Director General of Fine Arts ordered the reconstruction of the tower.

Siloé's work, as well as that of Jacobo Florentino, must be esteemed both for its architectural and sculptural aspects. From what was originally meant to be a humble Gothic church, they created one of the finest examples of Spanish Renaissance.

The polygonal sanctuary is decorated on the exterior with lovely cornices on the buttresses and sculptural groupings of giant Roman soldiers who bear the coats-of-arms of the founders. On the upper level there are two lovely figures representing Fortitude and Industry. They hold a large tablet which reveals the purpose of this monument. On it we read: «Gonzalo Fernández de Córdova great leader of the Spanish and terror of the French and the Turks». At each side there is a medallion with the portraits of El Gran Capitan and his wife.

These same themes were repeated indoors but they were unfortunately covered by XVIII century paintings.

On the domes of the transept and of the sanctuary, Siloé developed an iconographic work which glorifies the memory of the founders, buried in the church. In high relief he represents the heroes and heroines of antiquity, whose deeds he recalls and compares with those of El Gran Capitan and his wife. Here we see the figures of Caesar, Hannibal, Pompey, Mark, Homer and other heroines, as well as Abigail, Judith, Deborah, Penelope and other heroes.

On the coffers of the sanctuary's dome are represented the Savior, the Apostles, Angels and in relief there are several saints and the warrior saints. George, Sebastian, Martin and others. All this is featured in honour of El Gran Capitan and his wife.

Completing this monument is the Monastery of the same name with its two lovely cloisters, rich portals, and the coat-of-arms of the first archbishop of Granada, the monk Fray Hernando de Talavera, and of the Catholic Monarchs.

The most important sculptural piece of Andalusian Baroque art is the great «Retablo» of the main altar. It was contracted in 1570 to the painter Juan de Aragón who was assisted by the Granadine sculptor Melchor de Turín and the art studio of Vázquez el Joven. The design was modified in 1573 and amplified in 1603.

The whole of the Retablo, with its lovely gold tones completes the presbytery, offering us, as a whole, one of the loveliest images that XVII century Granada can offer.

There are many Renaissance portals of Mudejar churches in the city that bear the particular mark of Siloé's style. Clear examples of this are the portals of the churches of Santa Ana, S. Matias, el Salvador, S. Miguel, San Andres, S. Ildefonso and even the lovely building of the ancient University, today the Ecclesiastic Curia, closed because of a recent fire.

The Chancellory of Granada, work of Francisco del Castillo, with its rich historical legacy, closes and opens the transition from Renaissance to Baroque. It is, as a whole, but especially its facade, one of the most noble and monumental works of its time.

In 1500 the Catholic Monarchs initiated a judicial reform which included the transfer of one of the Royal Tribunals from Castille to Granada. By 1525 the available facilities proved inadecuate and the King decreed that a new residence should be built. Thus, this magnificent building with its imposing central patio, in which we find Siloé's influence, was built. The monumental stairway and the facade, however, were not begun until 1578 and 1587, respectively. By the end of the century the Chancellory was so well known in all of Spain that its beauty and originality were mentioned in literary works of the period.

The main entrance is topped by a sculptured marble slab, framed by a split pediment and supported by a lion. On it, in part, is inscribed in Latin: «May the Justice despensed herein be equal to the offense committed...». In the center and completing the façade is the Royal coat-of-arms, and at its sides and resting on the divided pediment are the statues of Justice and Fortitude.

Theodor Van Holland

Inmaculated Conception is the masterpiece of Alonso Cano as sculptor. Realized between 1652 and 1656 for the choir she has been ed in the sacristy for a better admiration.

Main façade of the Cathedral. Designed by Alonso Cano in 1667. On four pilasters are mounted three triumphant arches in Baroque chiaroscuro. The sculptures and the central medallion are the work of Risueño the rest done in the XVIII century are the work of Verdiguier.

When evaluating this facade we should mention the original distribution of the openings. All seems to be vertically linked, a fact which is accented by the contrast of the beveled stone with the flat stone. Contrasting the seven vertical groupings are the two horizontal cornices, one halfway with a small projection and the other at the top with a greater overhang. These cornices accentuate the semi-circular and triangular pediments of the seven balconies. All of the other openings including the first floor windows offer us with their curves and counter-curves a clear indicative of a pre-baroque style, also evident in the rich chromatic effect produced by the mixtures of grey, white and green marble.

The monumental nature of this building was justified because of the function it performed, as well as the history of this institution, which administered justice in Andalucia from 1505 to 1834.

In general, this solemn building sets before the plaza which is in front of it an image that clearly speaks of the greatness of Renaissance and baroque Granada. A period which was to be completed with other great baroque portals, retablos and altar niches such as the Diputación, the Law School (originally the Jesuit school of San Pablo), the Notary College and the churches of St. Justo and S. Pastor or of S. Juan de Dios or the Basilica of Nuestra Señora de las Angustias.

92

Dome of the Main Chapel. Our attention is centered on the ribs of the central dome which is illuminated by double row of stained glass windows with scenes of the redemption. The twelve pillars represent the twelve apostles.

D. Siloe (Capilla Mayor)

Sacristía

Detail of the Sacristy of la Cartuja and part of one of the inlaid doors, by Vázquez.

Preceding page: Sacristy of the Cartuja of Granada outstanding work of baroque art, where light, perspective, colour and materials produce impressive effects. First half of the XVIII century. Realized based on the ideas of Francisco Hurtado Izquierdo.

THE
CARTHUSIAN MONASTERY

T he monastery of la Cartuja, with its church, tabernacle, sacristy and other dependencies, is the monument which most clearly express- es what the Baroque style was in Granada. Founded in 1492 at the time of the Reconquest, it contains examples of Gothic, Renaissance and Plate- resque; but all that which is done in Baroque style, du- ring the XVII and XVIII centuries, is that which attains a superior level of quality, and within Spanish Baro- que, great originality. In many ways this can be consi- dered the culmination of Andalucian Baroque and the most profound and expressive example of religious ascetism and misticism in the life of the Carthusian monks.

In order to fully understand what this monument means in the life of the Order, one must first have an understanding of its location and surroundings. Out- side of the city, it is but a kilometre from the Puerta de Elvira and in a place where nature brimmed with beauty. During the reign of the Moors it was a place of orchards, carmenes (granadine villas), and many vine- yards, with abundant water from the fountains of Alfa- car. It was a fertile land with flourishing gardens as

described by Ibn Aljatib. It was a beautiful landscape covered with gardens. Today our imagination must take flight because of the great urban aspect of the surrounding area. The enclosed property of the monastery, however, allows us to imagine the once lovely gardens that were housed there.

According to a XVII century historian, this spot was chosen for the monastery as a result of an inicial con- tribution made by el Gran Capitan. It appears that he was at this spot when defending himself against the moors and he later expressed his desire to be buried here in a church.

First located on a hill it presented many difficulties to the first Carthusian builders, so much so that it was moved to an area of lower ground. As a result of this move El Gran Capitan became disinterested in the project and left it in the hands of the founders.

The move was approved in 1514 and the work was left in the hands of Fray Alonso de Ledesma, who pro- jected the dependencies around a great cloister, 53 metres long, with a cemetery in the center, then a lar- ge garden and a Claustrillo (little cloister), which is the one that exists today. Around this Claustrillo was pla-

Claustro

Baroque claustrillo and in the background the church of the monastery of La Cartuja, one of the most outstanding works of Spanish baroque from the XVII and XVIII centuries with works by the paintor Sánchez Cotán, Pedro Atanasio Bocanegra and the great Antonio Palomino, author of the paintings in the dome of the Sanctuary.

ced the Refectory, the Chapter House, the «Profundis» chamber and small chapels. Around the large Cloister were built the monks cells which no longer exist.

The church, affirms professor Orozco Díaz, was erected upon a foundation made in the XVI and XVII centuries by the quarrier Cristóbal de Vilchez. The Claustrillo was made at the same time and completed during the first quarter of the XVII century. According to the Carthusian historian José de Valles, four towers were planned, two at the foot and two at the head, of which only the one at the right of the epistolary was completed. It seems that it was a later idea to construct the Chapel of the Sagrario in the center of the sanctuary, as well as the great sacristy which was connected to the left of the same. At the end of the XVIII century in 1794, the Neoclassic portal is made, the work of the Hermoso brothers, Joaquín the architect and Pedro Antonio the sculptor of San Bruno in white marble.

At the back of an ample courtyard, which is reached through a Plateresque doorway, attributed to Juan García de Prades, is the majestic façade of the church, high atop a broad double Baroque staircase.

The sober Neoclassic portal, of grey marble stands out upon the honey coloured stone of the rest of the façade. Atop the entrance, as a royal foundation, is the coat-of-arms of Spain. Contrasting with this cultured image is the granadine stone pavement of the courtyard, covered with hunting scenes and the shield of Spain with the date 1679.

THE CLAUSTRILLO AND ITS SECTIONS

Today's entrance to the Monastery is through the claustrillo, just a simple patio with arches and with columns from the Doric style, open to the garden adn whose focal point is a fountain. A modern and well done restauration left it open, so creating a monastic atmosphere fitting in with the functions carried out in the XVII century, because in this way, the Refectory, the De Profundis, the Friars Chapter, the Monks Chapter and the north side, a series of chapels for intimate prayer and meditation, and the two doors to the church, all communicate with it.

For these sections —Claustrillo and the attached rooms— built in the XVI century and of gothic style with lovely ribbed vaults, expansive spaces harmoniously proportioned, Juan Sánchez Cotán drew a true chronicle of the Order; he was a laybrother of the Fraile Chapter, born in Orgaz in the province of Toledo in 1560 where he became a painter together with the manneristic naturalistic Blas de Prado, and who had come to this Cartuja in 1603. Near his works we find another series, also in the form of a chronicle, of the painter Vicente Carducho, replicas of those which he painted for the

Monasterio del Paular. All of them represent the history of the Order, from the death of Diocres in Paris, which motivated in St. Bruno and his companions the decision to establish the Order, —and that Sánchez Cotán painted in memory of the burial of the Lord of Orgaz of the Greco— up to the martyrdom scenes suffered by the monks in England during the epoch of Enrique VIII and in other parts of Europe at the hands of the Turks and the Huguenots.

The naturalism of the paintings, especially those by Sánchez Cotán, intentionally fill these silent spaces and invite the characters to emerge from their canvases, with their beautiful white robes in order to assist the Chapter and attend to the call of the church bells. So they become true illustrations of the live architectural texts and the monastic life, because they were painted for very concrete places of these sections; it is through them and through their apparent realism that we can see their trascendental idealism. Daily, the monks who prayed, studied and worked in this monastery, were able to realize their "visible talking". Such is the case of the presence of the first community of Christ with his apostles in the Last Supper, painted in the Refectory around 1618 and where the light projected above the cenacle equals the real light which penetrates through the lateral windows and illuminates and casts shadows on the abstinent dishes that are on the table. Another example is the representation of the martyr's exemplary heroism who die defending their faith, showing and example of value and confidence in God. In these sense, the bithematic and narrative canvases have a special didactic value, now grouped in the Refectory and Chapter rooms, some of them related to the life of St. Bruno and others to these martyrdom scenes.

It is probably here where Sánchez Cotán made one of the first monastic painting collections in Spain. A chapter which, during the XVII century, was abundant especially In Andalucía where the religious orders looked for, in these realistic series of deeds of a saint or merits of an order, the ideal ocassion to estimulate their own life of prayer and meditation in the monastic interiors. The paintings, which were destined to the walls of the convent, were big canvases and not frescos made for covering great spaces. For this reason, as the professor Julian Gallego noted, "when these canvases are taken from the place for which they were concieved and the displayed isolated in museums —as has happened with some of them— they cease to express the intention of its authors. It is certain that in these monastic collections there is a programmatic, didactic and even rethoric idea, which inspires the election and arrangements of the themes". Thus, each painting is valued not only by itself, but in relation with the rest of the series, and each series is articulateley explained in the entire house.

Nowadays, the series in the Cartuja of Granada —except those transferred to the Bellas Artes museums— are gathered in the Refectory Room, where the bithematic canvases dedicated to the martyrdoms works of Sánchez Cotán area highlighted; in the Chapter Room, the **Aparición de la Virgen a St. Bruno** on his deathbed, the miracles of his sepulcre and other works by Vicente Carducho are the focal point. In De Profundis Room, which served as prayer and mortuary chapel built in 1600 next to the Refectory, the friar laybrother painted and altarpiece with the figures of St. Peter and St. Paul and a landscape in the background; all of it showing a wide display of relief and visual effects, being both characteristics very common in the paintings at the end of the manneristic and the begginnings of the naturalistic periods. This tendency is also evident in the simple wooden cross, which with a minute detail of realism, the author has painted over the Last Supper in the Refectory Room. These "trompe l'oeil" were common in the paintings of the Cartujas.

In the small chapels of the north side are found two important pieces of the Baroque art of Granada. One of them is an impressive Ecce Homo, in multi-coloured fired clay; it is a work of the García brothers —Miguel and Jerónimo— at the end of the XVI century, a half torso, to be contemplated and meditated closely in the intimacy of a small chapel (this work didn't belong to the Cartuja). The other piece, a lovely image of the Virgen del Rosario by Jose Risueño, shows with a natural expression a beautiful Child in her arms who smilingly faces the onlooker. The certainly are two pieces that justify not only the function of intimate space in the baroque chapel, but also their own level of naturalism presente in the works that here fulfilled a function of real and bodily nearness to the image of the sacred. For these chapels Sánchez Cotán also painted some canvases, today in the Museum and in private collections, according to the affirmations of professor Orozco Díaz the author of an important unedited monography on the painter.

THE CHURCH

The Church, composed of only one groundplant, was erected in the XVII century by Cristóbal de Vílchez. The profuse decoration of its walls with plastered motifs of rich vegetation, producers impressions of spacial dynamism, accentuated with exhalted baroquism by the presence of zenithal light which contrast with the rhythm and reliefs; another factor is the predominant whiteness of the group only matched with the colours in the canvas of the series about the Life of the Virgin, painted in 1676 especially for this temple by the painter Pedro Atanasio Bocanegra of Granada, a disciple of Alonso Cano.

As a Carthusian church, its floor space is divided into three parts, each one according to a type of attendants: the first one is for believers in general, in the middle is the choir for the monks; these divisions don't interrupt the overall spacial continuity of the temple; the first part is separated by a simple metal grill, and the separation of the choirs is done with a lovely combination of two low retables with a glass and marquetery door, a work of the brother Vázquez. In such a way, all the decorative and figurative elements accentuate a rhythm which focuses towards the head where a baldachin altar, graceful and brilliant with gold and mirrors, is highlighted. it was made in 1710 by Francisco Hurtado Izquierdo with a image of the Asunción carved by José de Mora, supple and looking upwards. This combination communicates to the inside of the temple a high level of dynamism which transforms the ambience into something etherial and sublime. At the back, iconographically represented is the mistery of the Asunción de la Virgen on two canvases. Below, the apostles next to the vacant sepulcher, and above in the arcade of the ellipsoidal cupola the triunphant representation of the Virgin, lifted by the angels towards the heavens. The intensity of the presbytery colours makes the focal point even more attractive and transforms it into the point where everything converges. The space occupied by the Shrine, as the main chapel, centers in its darkness a background that becomes concave by its own transparency.

Together with this sensation of dynamism also abounds the impression of wealth which is greatly contributed by the two beautiful side retables made in the XVII century with canvases of Sánchez Cotán. On the right the Baptism of Christ and on the left The Rest on the Flight to Egypt; this last work is one of the finest belonging to the first epoch of the painter, and where the elegance and sobriety of the composition is accompanied by the fine treatment of the pictorial thematic

especially manifested in the still life where some bread and cheese are placed on a white tablecloth spread on the flowered covered grass, everything singing of the beauty and the trascendent contents of nature itself, which, as the poet affirms, is not dead here.

Completing the presbytery and at the end of the left side of the monks choir, is a beautiful retable (between 1730-1736) framing a canvas of the Virgen del Rosario by Pedro Atanasio Bocanegra and which reigns over the monks devotion in the choir and which artistically is the most expressive and communicative work of the disciple of Cano.

BAROQUISM AND SYMBOLISM IN THE SHRINE OF HURTADO IZQUIERDO

The overall attraction which the monument offers, as a monastic ambient for silence and meditation, arrives to its most important chapter with the execution of this singular piece of the Spanish Baroque and which is the Sanctum Sanctorum of the Cartuja. It seems, according to the known records, that the idea of its construction was probably decided in the middle of the XVII century and before finishing the decoration of the church because the presbytery's ornamental distribution alludes and frames the entrance to the interior of this new space that becomes the authentic nucleus, the center and final point of the whole cult of the temple; it also becomes one of the most exalted examples of the Spanish Baroque, magnificent in its movements and gestures and at the same time in harmony with the ensemble thanks to the plastic and colourful mobility of the different arts here represented in a pleasing harmony due to the creative idea and the deep argumental contents integrated in the whole.

The architectural structure was iniciated in 1702 according to the project and direction of the famous architect Francisco Hurtado Izquierdo, from the city of Lugo, and already known for his important works in Cordoba. The simplicity of the floor plan is resolved with a square which resting on four arches holds a cupola placed over trapezoidal pechinas together with lateral chapels which in ther turn reinforce and complete it; once in the interior there is an extremely beautiful conjunction of the supportive and decorative elements with an unique profusion of rich marbles, bright golden carvings, luminous frescos and oil paintings together with the iconographic and dynamic compliment of naturalistic sculptures which complete the architectonic plastic.

Everything here is in the state of effervescence, dynamisized in the structures and decorative surfaces. Nothing remains static, and for a more intense call to the senses, it seems as if the law of physics was inverted and the sustaining elements, the eight columns which occupy the four square angles and are mounted on complicated baroque styled plinths were hiding with their dark tones in front of the brilliant golds of the bases and capitals. The vertical repetition of its fluted shafts is in contrast with the curved profiles of the sculptures placed among them and even more with the pavillions which lodge them crowned bu angels who with their chromatism and ingravity contribute to their continous contrast. All the mouldings of the entablature, the frames of the paintings and the base of the cupola are outlined with ondulating lines, which dynamize even more the already existing mouldings.

Centering in the lateral sides, on the bottom parts, are open intrepid oculos which connect with the two chapels, framed by curves and non-curves of spirals and mouldings, sculptured in polished red marble, over which are placed the sis allegories, wood carved and richly polychromed in matt

St. Jerónimo.

Rodríguez Gutiérrez de Ceballos, whom we follow in this description— a small branch of alberchiqus in his hand, a consecrated bush in the ancient times to Hippocrates, the god of silence. Corresponding to this allegory an interpretation of the scene of Christ in the house of Martha and Martha is offered, insisting on Martha being the symbol of silence in the contemplative life.

The allegory of Solitude, situated in fromt of Silence, is a clear reference to life in the cell; here it is represented by a matron dressed in white with a solitary bird on her head, a book in her right hand for study and meditation and under her left arm a hare, an example of a solitary animal. In connection with this allegory Palomino has painted a medallion with the supper of Emaus a reference to the Eucharist and the lonely life of the withdrawn disciples and pilgrims. Finally, the four pechinas are occupied by the images of the four Evangelists.

All this program continues throughout the rest of the shrine, as much in the paintings as in the sculptures. In the entrance, the King-Prophet David is painted in the jambs; he is the ascendent of the Redemeer, and in his posture points towards the tabernacles; he also bears the palmist lire. In the opposite jamb Melchisedek is presented offering bread with both hands and a pitcher of wine at his feet, establishing a clear precedent of Jesus Christ's priesthood in relation to the Eucharist.

On the sides, next to one another, centered on the wall there are two enormous paintings also by Palomino both whith themes equally referring to the premonition and announcement of the Eucharist in the Old Testament. Thus, on the right side there is a scene which shows Moses with his prodigious staff, defending himself from the angel who is trying to kill his son with a sword; to avoid it, Sefora, his mother, circumcises him. Symbolically Moses represents Christ who has become the husband of the Church through the sacrifice of the Calvary which is renewed in the Eucharist. Above this painting the scene of David being given the sword of Goliath. In the lower part, sculptured, the allegories of the monastic virtues of the compunction with the mounth open and a heart crowned with thorns in the left hand and pointing to the heavens with the right. To its side, the virtue of Charity or the Love of God with a burning heart in its hand.

On the opposite wall there is also an Eucharisty prefiguration with the scene of Abigail offering to David gifts of bread, wine and a calf, so as to placate her anger against her husband Nabal. Above, the Purification de Isaías, known as the circumcision of the lips sculptured and on the pedestal are the allegories of the monastic virtues, done by Duque Cornejo; one of them is Obedience who bears a yoke in one hand and a crucifix in the other. At its side is Vigilance with a book in one hand and a lit candle in the other. At its side is a crane with the lifted claw sustaining a rock which doesn't allow him to fall asleep.

San Jerónimo

Obove some representative details of Siloé's style in the interior of the church.

de Ceballos, the symbolism of being the firts monastery cell for the Eucharist. Hidden and confined in the tabernacle. According to the pecualirity of the Carthusian life, here will be manifested the sumbols referring to a hermetical and cenobitical life, or to say, communal life and solitary life in the cell.

This main cell, symbolic and unique, is covered by a cupola where Palomino offers the triumphante celestial of the Eucharist in the exhalted monstrance —which here substitutes the Mystic Lamb— which here presides over the terrestial globe that St. Bruno holds as an atlantis. Palomino writes in conclusion: "By that token the whole recint becomes the expression of a militant church... and most especially is a panegyric of the holy Carthusian religion, based on the silence, contemplation and doctrine; these are the triumphant Jerusalem, represented in the Glory expressed in the entire ambient of the cupola; and thus, the inscences of this blessed community rise as the greatest gift to the Lords Sovereign".

On the base of the cupola, in painted figures and medallions, are represented a series of allegories and scenes referring to the Eucharist. The Faith, as the foundation of the Eucharistic mystery and the monastic life, is represented by a figure with a cartel which says, "Blessed are those who didn't see but believed" in relation to it, in the adjoining medallion, the historic institution, of the sacrament in the Last Supper: In Front of the Faith appears the Monastic Religion, represented as a grand matron with a veil over her face, carrying some cilices and disciplines. In relation to this allegory is the scene of Christ fasting in the desert and the subsequent help from the angels in regards to the Carthusian life and to the Eucharist.

The allegory of Silence is represented by and elder with his finger on his mounth and a quacking duch at his side, but the duck has a rock in its beak which prevents it from quacking. In addition this allegory of Silence has —according to P.

tones. All this monument of entrances and exits are compensed in his ground space with the small central, niche, who appears as a great marble monstrance, the axis and reason of the whole iconographic and dynamic content of this chapel, being the place to where everything converges and where originally was placed the primitive tabernacle, a beautiful urn made of bright silver a transparent crystal from where iniciates triumphantly and ascendent monument which as a fountain of bliss culminates firstly in the redempting cross, and lastly with the image of the Faith which seems due to the optic of the painting, to be embedded in the dome.

The conclusion is, as the Professor Orozco Díaz affirms, "that as in all the great baroque works, the most extraordinary Flattery and sensorial excitation, can take, by this way of the appearance of the senses to suggest the grandest and most transcendental religious spirit". But it happens that, inside all this language of the forms, integrated by the various arts, there is a complete iconographic and symbolic discourse which transforms this room into a beautiful synthesis of what it signifies for the Cartuja the cult of the Eucharist as the triumphant right where is manifested the love of God towards mankind. Palomino, painter of the cupola and of the paintings in the shrine, refers to it in his famous book Museo Pintorico y Escala Optica, but recently the works of Rene Taylor, Orozco Díaz and above all Rodríguez Gutiérrez de Ceballos, have insisted in this aspect which justifies this great work in the line defended by the Council of Trent, in its XXV session of 1563, the Faith. Should be expressed through images and paintigs for didactic and comprension reasons.

Morever, the Carthusian Order, since its General Chapter in 1261, ordered a special distribution of its churches in such a way that all its parts were to be in spacial and visual contact with the shrine, thus becoming the center of the cult. But the sumbology of the chapel of the shrine has, also here, in the Cartuja of Granada, according to Father Rodríguez Gutiérrez

On the far wall there is a window, with an important function in the lighting at the room. On both sides are the allegories of Peace and Gentleness, the first crowned with a laurel and the second with a meek lamb which substitutes the symbolic elephant, the most common attribute of this virtue.

In the central niche this symbolic-iconographic discourse is completed with four virtues and monastic qualifications which are: Veritas, with a rich diadem on his forehead and an open book; Integritas, with a tablet with Arabic numbers: Examen, with a clepsydra or a water clock, and Esca, or food, with a fish referring to the rigour of the fast and the abstinence fo Carthusian life. These virtues, are carved in wood, based on models by Duque Cornejo, and are richly polychromed in gold which makes them more dynamic and supple.

The four great figures which occupy the angular intercolumnation are St. Juan Bautista, by Risueño; La Magdalena by Duque Cornejo; St. Bruno and St. José by José de Mora, like wise complete this iconographic collection the first three representing the penitent and the anchorite life, and St. José as an example of a silent and secluded life.

Thus, and as conclusion, this magnificent baroque piece offers for its understanding two complementary discourses: a plastic one, with a dynamism of forms, lights and colours and the erudit and symbolic discourse whose manifestations give the image of the Eucharist triumph, and further more the symbolic cell, and Carthusian ideal for the Eucharistical Christ.

THE SACRISTY

Outside of the Sagrario and to the left of the presbytery we see before us doors of Taracea (inlaid with ivory, ebony and tortoise shell). An impressive spectacle of Andalusian Baroque architecture which creates fantastic effects of light and perspective.

On the 5th of January 1713 the construction of the

Sacristy was authorized and it is assumed that because of his success with El Sagrario, Francisco Hurtado Izquierdo also planned the first steps of the new work, although there is no record of who directed the project. The most important period was from 1741-1747 during which time all the interior stucco work, the three foot dado of veined brown marble and the paving were completed. There are many suppositions as to the masters who created this work but no document reveals with certainty its authors.

Once more, a key work in the history of art, both for its style, as well as its type, remains anonymous. This unique work, different from all others of the same type, such as the Sagrario of the church of S. Mateo by Leonardo Antonio de Castro or the Sagrario of the parish of Priego de Pedrajas.

Aesthetically, this work utilizes the effects of perspective and light. Space, illuminated from the sides or from above, make dynamic the chiaroscuro of the carved white adornments outlined in blue to project spaces and profiles. Everything seems to sprout from the veined and intensely contrasting marble of the dado. The pavement, in black and white diamond shaped marble, increases the dynamic space and seems to remove the background to a distance, creating an environment without static references.

This unreal world into which we are drawn is the perfect backdrop for appreciating the ecstasy of the small statue of St. Bruno by José de Mora. This unique example of plastic mysticism closes our visit to one of the most important chapters in Christian and Baroque Granada.

Domingo Sánchez Mesa
Professor of History of Art
University of Granada

The Monastery of St. Jerónimo, one of the principal Renaissance buildings in Granada mainly the work of Diego de Siloé its interior, —church and cloister—, is one of the finest examples of granadine art. This church is the burial place of El Gran Capitan Gonzálo Fernández de Córdoba.

On the Carrera del Darro, one of the loveliest areas of Granada, we find this palace today the provincial archeological museum. The faca of this palace de Castril is one of the richest plateresque facades in Granada. Attributed to Sebastián de Alcántara and dated 1539.

CASA DE ZAFRA (del Castril)

Cenete

Calahorra (Patio)

Bayárcal

Montefrío

El Charcón

Backcover: Central detail of the «reja» of the Royal Chapel, by Bartolomé el Rejero (1520). The coat-of-arms of Spain with the political symbols of the yoke and arrows between angels grotesque figures and lions. The detail work in iron en the richness of the polychromed colors and gilded are worth noting.